"Eye opening and inspiring, *Toge* [...] of the day, holds out a clear and [...] to see all church leaders read this, soak up its spirit, and rise to its challenge."
Michael Reeves, president and professor of theology, Union School of Theology, author of *Delighting in the Trinity*

"This book may be our best hope to move collaborative church planting from an oxymoron to the unstoppable force it was meant to be. What if whole cities joined together to start new churches that were making the gospel known in fresh ways to our increasingly post-Christian context? These words connect thought leadership with praxis to remind us that if the gospel is at the heart of our churches this truly is the way forward."
Nancy Ortberg, chief executive officer of Transforming the Bay with Christ

"Over the past ten years 2020birmingham has pioneered an innovative model of collaborative church planting that has borne much fruit and is now being replicated in other cities and regions around the United Kingdom. It is rooted in a determination to reach the lost, maintain faithfulness to the gospel, and build generous partnerships with those who share core convictions. Neil Powell and John James tell their exciting story with passion and humility. They set out a compelling vision for citywide gospel movements and provide practical guidance for their formation and functioning. It is impossible to read this book without aspiring to achieve more for Christ and the advancement of his kingdom in the place you live."
John Stevens, national director of Fellowship of Independent Evangelical Churches

"*Together for the City* is a rally cry for unity across denominations, networks, and movements in order to champion disciplemaking in our cities. Since the gospel changes people and people change the world, then we must do whatever it takes to strategically reach people in our cities. Neil Powell and John James are wise practitioners who graciously share their years of insights both locally and globally in this book. We must lock arms and partner together for the city, recognizing that we can surely do more together than we ever could on our own."
Dhati Lewis, lead pastor of Blueprint Church, Atlanta, vice president of the Send Network

"*Together for the City* is the most inspiring book I've read all year. It's amazing to think what God might do if churches and pastors work together to see movements of God in their cities. Imagine what would happen if church leaders collaborated together across denominational lines to see new churches started for the glory of God. The fruit would be immeasurable. I can't wait to apply the concepts and practices from this book in my own context."
Dave Furman, senior pastor, Redeemer Church of Dubai, author of *Being There* and *Kiss the Wave*

"A passionate call for evangelical collaboration in church planting for the sake of the gospel. This is good news indeed for our city."
The Right Reverend David Urquhart KCMG, The Lord Bishop of Birmingham

"God has beautifully designed us for community and this community is also expressed and experienced in our mission that God, by grace, has called us to. Neil Powell and John James will challenge you to think big. They will share helpful, practical concepts and tools, and they will leave you inspired to not only think of planting one or two churches but also envision a movement that plants healthy gospel churches for your city and beyond."

One Mokgatle, network director for Southern Africa, Acts 29

"In our current cultural moment, the urgency of our missionary calling necessitates us breaking free from a tethering tribalism. Gospel churches, gospel people, and gospel leaders *need* each other and *need* to collaborate. In *Together for the City*, Powell and James are able to tell us their particular story in their particular city in a way that acts as an exemplar for your particular story in your particular city. It's illuminating, inspiring, and for tribal folk, quite unsettling—but we do need to hear it and act on it!"

Daniel Strange, director, Oak Hill College

"Do you have a burden to reach your city with the gospel? And do you realize that you can't do it on your own? If so, then you've picked up the right book! Neil and John present a well-worn path that will help you move from isolation to collaboration so that you can—together with others—plant churches that plant churches. Don't miss this important work that should be standard for every church planter and pastor moving forward."

Daniel Im, pastor, podcaster, and author of *Planting Missional Churches*

"Praise God for this inspiring, challenging, useful, and timely book. . . . It's time we worked out how to cooperate without being too broad nor too narrow, in order to reach the vast numbers of people around us who are drowning in sin. I have admired God's work in Neil Powell and in 2020birmingham and in City to City for many years, *soli Deo gloria.*"

Richard Coekin, executive director of Co-Mission, London

"There is a new wind of God blowing across the Christian landscape, and it is forging a unique and beautiful unity among churches and movements. In this book, the authors succeed in showing the practical outworking of such collaboration, its benefit to the city, and the kingdom expansion it brings through church planting. This is a much-needed model of mission partnership."

Tope Koleoso, lead pastor of Jubilee Church London

"With a solid, biblical foundation, the authors encourage meaningful gospel collaboration among local churches of all different stripes, but who agree on core doctrinal truth. This book exudes a sense of purpose, joy, and local intentionality in mission. It will challenge and encourage in equal measure, as it shows how partnerships, though at times uncomfortable, can bear much gospel fruit."

Steve Timmis, CEO, Acts 29

Together for the City

NEIL POWELL
and JOHN JAMES

Foreword by
TIMOTHY KELLER

**How Collaborative
Church Planting
Leads to Citywide
Movements**

An imprint of InterVarsity Press
Downers Grove, Illinois

InterVarsity Press
P.O. Box 1400, Downers Grove, IL 60515-1426
ivpress.com
email@ivpress.com

InterVarsity Press® is the book-publishing division of InterVarsity Christian Fellowship/USA®, a movement
of students and faculty active on campus at hundreds of universities, colleges, and schools of nursing in the
United States of America, and a member movement of the International Fellowship of Evangelical Students.
For information about local and regional activities, visit intervarsity.org.

All Scripture quotations, unless otherwise indicated, are taken from The Holy Bible, New International
Version®, NIV®. Copyright © 1973, 1978, 1984, 2011 by Biblica, Inc.™ Used by permission of Zondervan.
All rights reserved worldwide. www.zondervan.com. The "NIV" and "New International Version" are
trademarks registered in the United States Patent and Trademark Office by Biblica, Inc.™

While any stories in this book are true, some names and identifying information may have been changed to
protect the privacy of individuals.

Cover design and image composite: David Fassett
Interior design: Jeanna Wiggins
Images: satellite view of Cleveland, Ohio: © Stocktrek / DigitalVision / Getty Images
    white marble texture: © undefined undefined / iStock / Getty Images Plus
    Chicago skyline: © Yousef Alkh / EyeEm / Getty Images

ISBN 978-0-8308-4153-0 (print)
ISBN 978-0-8308-6564-2 (digital)

Printed in the United States of America ∞

Library of Congress Cataloging-in-Publication Data
A catalog record for this book is available from the Library of Congress.

P 21 20 19 18 17 16 15 14 13 12 11 10 9 8 7 6 5 4 3 2 1

Y 37 36 35 34 33 32 31 30 29 28 27 26 25 24 23 22 21 20 19

For Jane and Sarah

and our fellow church planters who

make up 2020birmingham

Without you this story could not be told

Contents

A Bigger Vision

Timothy Keller

The book before you is an exciting project. I've known one of its authors, Neil Powell, for a number of years, and I regard him as one of the most important leaders of the evangelical church in Britain. Neil was one of the first there to answer the call that Redeemer City to City has been issuing for citywide church-planting movements. I had made the case for movements like these in *Center Church*, my book describing a vision for gospel-centered, city-centered, and movement-centered ministry. Now, that vision has been realized in 2020birmingham, the remarkable church network that Neil has seen grow in an urban center in England. 2020birmingham is an embodiment of Redeemer City to City's theory and vision and is one of the most successful ministry projects in all of Europe.

Here Neil and John James, his fellow member of 2020birmingham and partner in writing this book, present an instructive and inspiring case study of ministry in the UK's second city. They build on that history to offer both a vision and practical resources so gospel-believing churches in any city can mount the same kind of movement.

First, the authors show how the vision for collaborative church planting comes from "a great need for the gospel." Most see the world as divided between good people and bad people. The good (the moral or the liberal or the conservative—or just the people like "us") are making the world a better place, while those "others" are ruining things. So we think we need to liberate the good folks and marginalize the bad ones. The gospel, by contrast, provides both a far more dire and a far more hopeful assessment of the world's situation. Everyone, nice and nasty, is spiritually blind and eternally lost. All our problems stem from sin and the resulting breakdown of all relationships. In your city, the respectable are as lost and as affected by sin as the criminals and prostitutes on the streets. And yet the Bible promises that God's kingdom and gospel will triumph in the end. So the need for the gospel is massive, and the gospel's prospects are even greater.

This means that Christian leaders can't be satisfied with the status quo. Ministers are often called "stewards" in the Bible (1 Corinthians 4:1-2; 1 Peter 4:10 ESV), and the master of the house in the parable of the talents assumed that his stewards would not merely keep his assets safe but also invest in order to increase them (Matthew 25:14-30). The point isn't about money, but that we have the mysteries of God: the gospel (1 Corinthians 4:1-2; Colossians 1:26-27). And we know what God wants us to do with the gospel. He sends us out in an ever-expanding mission to disciple the nations (Acts 1:8; 8:4; 8:26-40; 10; Matthew 28:18-20). So no church should exist just to keep its doors open and maintain things. The master condemned the laziness of the steward who only conserved his assets (Matthew 25:26).

This parable can't be turned into a wooden insistence that every congregation keep growing in numbers. Sometimes faithful preaching shrinks the numbers of an unhealthy church, and there are plenty of other good reasons why an individual congregation may remain at its size. The parable means that the church leaders of a whole city or region can't rest content. They must strive to further the mission of Jesus with the resources they've been given. They must cast vision for reaching the city together.

It's natural for a human organization to begin as a movement (coming into existence to further a cause outside itself), but most eventually become tribes (existing mainly to serve themselves and the interests of their members). Biblical steward-leadership offers a built-in resistance to this natural trend. The steward must not let the household operate and exist for the interests of those in power within it. The steward's job is to work for the interests of the Master. God punishes stewards who use his assets for their own comfort (see, for example, Luke 12:45-47). The Lord gives us his Word and Spirit and expects us to multiply his resources for his glory.

Even if a set of churches holds basic theological truths and doctrines of the biblical gospel in common, it's very challenging to cooperate across the barriers of denomination and tradition. All should agree that Jesus called the church to be one for the purpose of a unified witness before the world (John 17:20-21). So as long as this doesn't entail doctrinal compromise, it's a worthy goal. Nevertheless, very few leaders are confident that these barriers can be overcome. Many question the possibility and therefore the wisdom of even trying.

In *Together for the City,* the authors show that the resources for practical collaboration in cities lie in the gospel itself, particularly in the generosity and humility that a true grasp of the gospel always produces.

When the disciples saw someone who wasn't a member of their band ministering "in Jesus' name," they tried to stop him "because he was not one of us" (Mark 9:38). Jesus was far more generous in replying, "Whoever is not against us is for us" (9:40). At that point, the disciples didn't understand the gospel. When Peter fell back into eating only with Jewish Christians and not with Gentile Christians, Paul told him he was forgetting the gospel of justification by grace alone through faith alone (Galatians 2:14). How, Paul argued, can you think you're better than anyone else when you know you're equally sinful and lost before God, yet saved by sheer grace and justified by Christ's work, not your own?

If we only give lip service to the gospel, not grasping it and rejoicing in it, a proud and ungenerous spirit will stymie any collaboration with others who also minister in Christ's name. When we look for justification—even unconsciously—in our doctrinal distinctives, we will not be humble; we will look down on those who do not share our tradition. If we subtly look for justification in our ministry successes, we won't be generous. It will become impossible to share power and to sacrifice time and money that could be used to build our own ministry's size and status. But the gospel gives us both the vision and the resources to work together to reach our cities.

For the sake of the world mission of the church, churches and Christian leaders must unite within their cities across tribal barriers in order to increase the number of disciples and churches. While there is an increasing body of literature about church planting in general, there is almost nothing available that describes whole-city collaboration among multiple denominations, networks, and movements. Neil and John spell out what it takes to get this done. I know of no better book on the subject.

The Bigger Picture

Through a Wide-Angle Lens

Many of us at Crossway Church knew James was unwell, but he had played it down. He looked jaundiced and became breathless quickly. Not until the Macmillan nurse[1] began to visit did I (John) realize just how serious the problem was. And I was in Queen Elizabeth Hospital, sitting by his bed, guitar in hand, trying to sing "Mighty to Save" and hold it together.

Friendship with James was a life's ministry in microcosm. He had lived most of his adult life with the traveling community before returning to a hostel in Birmingham.[2] It was then that an old school friend invited him to church, assuring him we were "not like other churches." I first met James when he arrived like a whirlwind at our Sunday-morning gathering. Later we began to read Mark's Gospel together, and he became convinced of the good news of Jesus, heard the call to repent and believe, and became a Christian. He was baptized and welcomed into membership, and he threw his all into the youth clubs and building maintenance team.

James began to grow and change. He was increasingly reconciled to his family. He was increasingly able to control his temper. He was increasingly using the gifts God had given him. And then his health deteriorated—quickly. It was eighteen months from born again to final breath.

So, picture the scene. A new creation, a beautiful child of God, rescued from chaos and darkness, saved from the judgment to come, is lying on a hospital bed during his final week on the wrong side of glory. The church pastor is way out of his depth, bumbling his way through James's favorite worship song, holding back the tears, and attempting to speak the comforting words of the gospel.

But then zoom out, and you'll see two other church members, also recent converts, holding James's hand, quietly praying, trying to make their way through the song too. You'll see three other church members making their way along the corridor, preparing themselves to sit and pray, to tell jokes, to shed tears.

Widen the angle again, and you'll see an entire church family gathering under God's Word. They are praying together for James in the building he helped to maintain, nestled in the heart of a large council estate on the south side of the city of Birmingham.[3] You will see a small, multigenerational, multiethnic community that rejoices with those who rejoice and mourns with those who mourn. You will see a youth group of more than forty primary-age local children diligently making "get well soon" cards as they have the news about one of the youth club team sensitively explained to them.

But then pan out further, and you'll see that this church family is the fruit of a seven-year church revitalization project, with a core team willing to plant into a dying church that had given itself just a couple of years to wind down and close. You'll see a welcoming faithful remnant girding their loins for the challenges that will follow. You'll see men and women, young and old, walking along the way of the cross through a process of costly change in order to recover a frontier for mission and begin to make disciples again.

Now zoom out further still. If you look carefully, you'll glimpse 2020birmingham, a diverse coalition of about twenty local churches collaborating in order to see this revitalization happen. You'll see other church-planting initiatives across the city, each taking a different form and reaching a different context. You'll see established churches willing to give away their best people to join core teams, willing to give time to pray, willing to give from their budgets to get things off the ground, and willing to counsel young church leaders who are way out of their depth. You'll see churches willing to cross boundaries to partner with others in order to reach Birmingham for Jesus, believing they can do more together than they can on their own. This is the bigger picture.

Why We Have Written This Book

We have a deep conviction that the more willing we are to find ways to collaborate, the more effective we'll be in reaching our city for Jesus. The more generous we are toward one another, the more God will bear fruit through us. The closeup and the bigger picture of the opening scene are connected. This is life and death, and heaven and hell. It's what gets us out of bed in the morning. The need is too great to allow our vision to be too small. Without 2020birmingham, the Crossway Church described above would not have undergone revitalization. For James, in the providence of God, a bigger vision made the difference for eternity.

We aim to convince you that collaborative church-planting movements are a Christ-honoring implication of the gospel and a strategic way to reach our communities for Jesus.

We aim to cast the bigger vision by telling our story as transparently as we can and by introducing you to what is happening all over the world. If God can use us in this way, he can use anyone.

In a way that may be useful to you in your context, we aim to share our experiences with you as well as some of the convictions we have grown in, lessons we have learned, and principles we have discovered.

We aim to encourage you wherever you are on this journey and to implore you to see that we each have a role to play in this bigger vision—for the sake of people like James.

With a vision to reach lost people through church planting and with healthy collaboration at its heart, by the grace of God may we together reach our cities—and through them, the world.

Who We Are Writing For

You may already be convinced of the need for collaborative church-planting movements. You are ready to go, and you hope we can help you get started. Our prayer is that this book will be a practical encouragement to get you on your way.

Or you may be unconvinced and are wondering why this should be a priority for ministry. Perhaps you're struggling to see how to embrace collaboration without compromise. Perhaps you assume this kind of vision is for bigger or more established churches than yours. Almost certainly you're already far too busy and are wondering why this should take up valuable space. Our prayer is that *Together for the City* will be a provocative book that prompts you to think again.

Ideally we're writing for people who are open to the idea but need to be equipped to defend it among those who are more skeptical. There is a difficult balance. Perhaps you instinctively "get it." We hope we get practical enough quickly enough, and that the time spent defending principles helps root your convictions. Perhaps you're reading with the voice of a cautious leadership team in your ears. We hope that we've done enough groundwork to aid you with difficult conversations. We also hope that our story will give you confidence to step out with risky faith.

It's also possible that our talk of "the city" is a barrier to you. You picture a large metropolis and struggle to relate that image to your context. Throughout the book, "the city" is simply any local conurbation. Across the world, what defines a city varies significantly. In Scandinavia, urban populations may be as low as a few hundred people, whereas in the United States, they begin in the thousands. In the United Kingdom, large towns with cathedrals are called cities, regardless of size. Please don't let the word *city* put you off or alienate you if you wouldn't define your own locality as a city. This principle remains: the more open we are to collaboration, the more effectively we can reach our community. This is what it means to be together for the city.

Introducing the Authors

Twenty years ago, when I (John) was a student, I joined a local church in Birmingham where Neil was the student worker. A year later Neil co-led the planting of a new church in the city, and I followed. We met and read Mark's Gospel together at eight-thirty every Friday morning in the first year of the church plant. I became the first ministry trainee at the church, and later on, as 2020birmingham was conceived, I returned to the city to lead a church revitalization project, mentored by Neil.

We've worked side by side since the conception of 2020birmingham. Neil is a key catalyst for the group, and I talk with churches about revitalization. Neil is primarily the movement's brains, while I am primarily the writing brawn. So this book reflects the movement's spirit; collaboration has helped us do what was beyond each of us alone.

We want to be careful not to exaggerate the progress of 2020birmingham or to claim more than reality would allow. We aren't sure whether what we belong to could be described as a movement yet. 2020birmingham exhibits movement dynamics and has the potential to develop into a full-blown one. However, spiritual movements aren't manufactured by human ingenuity, but instead rest on the sovereign work of the Holy Spirit. Throughout the book, we are careful to say that 2020birmingham is a fledgling movement. Our prayer to our heavenly Father is that what he has begun may grow into something that truly allows him to work powerfully among us and through us, for the sake of his Son's glory and our lost city.

How This Book Is Organized

Together for the City has three parts. Part one, "Why and What," makes the case for localized collaborative church-planting movements, why we think they are necessary, and what they look like. Part two, "How," works through a formula for creating collaboration with integrity. In part three, "Who," we seek to show you how you may play a part in coming together for your city. We'll also share some of the lessons we've been learning and offer a number of examples from around the world.

Part one: Why and What. In chapter one, "Vision," we explain how the size of the spiritual need and the size of the opportunity have the power to compel us to a bigger vision—a vision on a scale that no single church could realize alone.

In chapter two, "Beginnings," we briefly chart the history of our local collaborative attempt to realize this vision.

In chapter three, "Movements," we draw out some healthy dynamics we believe have helped encourage the collaborative church-planting movement we're advocating.

Part two: How. In our experience, collaborative church-planting movements require three components that we express as the following formula: core + cause + code = collaboration.

In chapter four, "Core," we explain how a shared core of beliefs rooted in the gospel creates the boundary of orthodoxy for a movement. A movement must be defined by, remain rooted in, protect, and celebrate the core of the good news of Jesus.

In chapter five, "Cause," we explain how the common cause of a movement is established. We also explore the role theological vision plays in creating collaborations that exist to accomplish a clear purpose.

In chapter six, "Code," we identify the DNA that energizes and coheres a movement, unifying it, bringing it to life, and galvanizing it into action.

In chapter seven, "Collaboration," we explore the output of the equation: Christ-honoring collaboration. We sketch the types and degrees of collaboration that are possible within the context of a movement, demonstrating the way in which everyone can play a part. As we do, we recognize that movements look different from place to place and from person to person.

Part three: Who. In chapter eight, "Taking Part," we chart the growth of a movement from conception through to realization, encouraging you to see the part you may play as well as sharing some of the lessons we've learned in our own context.

In chapter nine, "Together Around the World," we include a number of case studies and reflections from others around the world who own a bigger vision for their context.

Together for the City

With a wide-angle lens, a picture becomes a story. Imagine a snapshot of a small child on an inflatable mattress, floating on water. It makes all the difference in the world if the context is the tranquility of the shallow end of a swimming pool or the tumult of the middle of the Atlantic Ocean. The bigger picture matters. The bigger picture tells the story. The bigger picture makes the difference between raising a smile and raising the alarm.

As twenty-first-century believers scattered throughout the world, would we describe our bigger picture as a pool of tranquility or a raging storm? Should we be buying ice creams or launching life-boats? The apostle Paul urges us, "Be very careful, then, how you live—not as unwise but as wise, making the most of every oppor-tunity, because the days are evil" (Ephesians 5:15-16). Right now, that is the wide-angle story.

Although we hope that in reading this book you smile from time to time, we seek to raise the alarm. The needs and opportunities demand a response that will be met only under God with a bigger vision. How do we make the most of every opportunity? We must be—and we can be—together for the city.

PART 1

Why and What

Vision

Church planting is good.

A vision for church multiplication is better.

ED STETZER

What this chapter is about:

- *why the gospel requires us to collaborate through church-planting movements;*
- *why the scale of spiritual need demands a size of vision for a locality that no single church, network, or denomination can realize alone; and*
- *why the gospel not only compels but also enables collaboration.*

We'll also outline five principles that are all implications of the good news of Jesus: fidelity, urgency, compassion, generosity, and humility. Together these enlarge our vision and make the case for the necessity of collaboration.

A Dunkirk Spirit

My (Neil's) uncle Reg is remembered particularly for two things: first, he was born on February 29, which meant missing a lot of birthdays. Second, he was a soldier rescued from Dunkirk during the Second World War.

In May 1940, German forces swept through Belgium and northern France in a blitzkrieg that left the British Expeditionary Force cornered with their backs against the coastline. The new prime minister, Winston Churchill, ordered Lord John Gort, the force's commander, to evacuate as many troops as possible back to Britain from the port of Dunkirk in France.

And so on May 20, Operation Dynamo was formulated. With the Nazis fast advancing, it was estimated that as many as forty-five thousand men might be successfully evacuated. On May 26, Britain held a national day of prayer, and King George VI attended a special service in Westminster Abbey. The Archbishop of Canterbury led prayers "for our soldiers in dire peril in France." Operation Dynamo began the next day.

On the first day, only 7,669 men were saved, and after two days, the total number had risen to twenty-five thousand, which was well below the target. Those in command enlarged the vision, and a call went out across the British Isles: all available sailing vessels, piloted by civilians, must head for Dunkirk and assist in the evacuation. By May 31, nearly four hundred small craft were voluntarily and enthusiastically engaged for the effort, and the rescue numbers began to rise. In response to the moment of national crisis, 933 ships sailed to Dunkirk: private yachts, motor launches, lifeboats, paddle steamers—anything that would float. Over a period of eight days, it was not just forty-five thousand that were rescued but 338,226, including my uncle Reg.

As Christians, we face a similar situation. Many people are in dire peril, and God's Operation Dynamo is underway. We sense the urgent need for action and are working hard at mobilizing our congregations to reach the lost. We run guest events and inquirers courses. We plan community projects and train in friendship evangelism. And all of these are wonderfully used by God to bring people into his kingdom. More churches than ever are grasping a vision for reaching out further through church planting, and yet these endeavors alone can't reach the full extent of the communities God has placed us in.

The population of the United Kingdom is currently growing by around half a million people every year, which is a growth rate of 0.8 percent. The church in the United Kingdom has a growth rate of negative 1.4 percent per year.[1] According to *Operation World*, the growth rate among evangelicals in the United Kingdom is estimated to be zero percent.[2] Across Europe as a whole, only 2.5 percent are estimated to be evangelicals, and the annual growth rate of Christians is negative 0.3 percent.[3] The population of the United States has a steady growth rate of 0.71 percent. And yet, according to historical theologian Albert Mohler, four thousand churches close their doors every year, with only one thousand evangelical churches being planted in their place.[4]

We are in dire peril. What does it mean for us to respond to the need and to enlarge the vision? What if a truly collaborative answer to the call is possible? What if there is a way for faithful churches across denominations, ecclesial styles, and theological traditions to partner in a rescue effort that would rival Operation Dynamo? This is the vision of a local collaborative church-planting movement.

We need a Dunkirk spirit, where a huge number of lifeboats were mobilized to realize a vision far too big for any group to achieve alone. The result was extraordinary—in fact, miraculous. It was a life-and-death effort, and Uncle Reg was saved because of it. In this chapter, we want to show how it's possible for churches to be mobilized to get as many boats as possible in the water, of all shapes and sizes—anything that will float—to rescue the lost.

One Local Vision: 2020birmingham

Allow us to introduce one local, fledgling attempt to be together for the city.

Birmingham is Europe's youngest city, with 38 percent of the population aged under twenty-five.[5] It is also the United Kingdom's second-largest city, with a population of more than 1.1 million people and 4.3 million living within an hour's commute of the center. It's an extraordinarily diverse city in which 57 percent of children under eleven are from a variety of ethnic minorities, and over a fifth of the population is Muslim.[6]

The city is growing by an average of two hundred people a week, but the church is not. Between 2005 and 2010, the population of Birmingham grew by more than 7 percent (more than seventy thousand people), and yet during the same period, the number of churches in the West Midlands increased by less than 0.5 percent—seven churches, to be precise. Ninety-four percent of people in the city are entirely unchurched or de-churched, yet it has grown into one of the United Kingdom's most religiously diverse conurbations.[7]

In Birmingham, a growing number of churches are seeking to see the bigger picture and find ways to work together to reach the city through church planting. 2020birmingham began in 2010 with a simple vision: to see twenty churches planted or revitalized by 2020. In the first year, there were just a handful of partners, one pioneer church plant, and a church revitalization project. But over the past eight years, we've witnessed seventeen new green shoots begin to grow.

We also have prayerfully reset the vision: please God, another thirty by 2030. If we can have the privilege of seeing fifty churches planted or revitalized in the Birmingham area, each with a love of church planting in their DNA, we may see one hundred in our lifetime.

2020birmingham was born out of the conviction that as churches we need to seek to reach the whole city. In comparison to the size of the challenge, we're a small group with modest aims, and yet our prayer is that God will use our endeavors for his glory and kick-start a movement. The goal is certainly not rooted in our competency, but in Christ. He has helped us to see that we can do more together than we could on our own, and we *must* if we are to see our city reached for him.

The churches actively collaborating to form 2020birmingham come from a number of different networks. New Frontiers, the Fellowship of Independent Evangelical Churches, Acts 29, Christian Brethren, the Baptist Union, and the International Mission Board are all represented within the group. Beyond this active core, a number of others are partnering in a supportive capacity, including Greater European Mission, Birmingham City Mission, and the Church of England.

Note that we aren't seeking to plant churches together but to be together as we plant churches. Significant distinctives set each of these groups apart from one another, but we are also united by a common burden and vision: to see the good news of Jesus flourish in our city. We recognize that unless we're willing to build bridges across denominational boundaries, we'll never see the advance of the gospel that we're longing for.

Only Halfway There: Why We Need a Bigger Vision

Because you've chosen to read this book, we expect that you're convinced of the lordship of Jesus, his glorious gospel of grace, his call to take up your cross and follow him, his commission to make disciples of all nations, and his means of doing that through local expressions of his body, the church, empowered by his Holy Spirit.

You are likely also to be convinced of the biblical imperative to belong to a church and even to pursue the planting of churches where the gospel is not known. You know that the heartbeat for world mission pulses throughout Scripture. The beautiful feet that bring good news do so that "all the ends of the earth will see the salvation of our God" (Isaiah 52:10). Even in the Old Testament, the good news of Yahweh has centrifugal force, pushing Israel to declare him to the whole world.[8] God loves all nations, as Jonah reluctantly acknowledged of the city of Nineveh, where the people couldn't "tell their right hand from their left" (Jonah 4:11). "I knew that you are a gracious and compassionate God, slow to anger and abounding in love" (4:2).

In the New Testament, this comes into sharp focus. Jesus responded to the criticism that he welcomed sinners and ate with them by telling three parables in which the lost are actively pursued and diligently sought and in which heaven rejoices when they are found. The punchline of this whole section of Luke's Gospel is Jesus' summary of his mission "to seek and to save the lost"; these are the lost of "all nations" (Luke 19:10, 24:47), those whom missiologists today call "every people group and population segment."[9]

This then becomes the mission of the church, empowered by the Holy Spirit. Jesus promises his disciples, "You will receive power when the Holy Spirit comes on you; and you will be my witnesses in Jerusalem, and in all Judea and Samaria, and to the ends of the earth" (Acts 1:8). The church began in Jerusalem, and when even the opposition acknowledged that this fledgling community had filled Jerusalem with their teaching (5:28), the scattering of God's people and message to Judea and Samaria commenced in the providence of God (8:1). The church in

Antioch was founded, and from there the missionary journeys and the planting of churches to the ends of the earth began. The world still cries out with the man of Macedonia, "Come over . . . and help us" (16:9). And we must respond with anything that will float.

Our prayer is that you may be convinced of all these things, if you aren't already. However, a deeper, more sustained reflection on the gospel calls us to be part of a *bigger* vision. Even if we're convinced of the gospel, convinced of the need for gospel ministry, convinced of the necessity of the local church, convinced of the need to plant churches, we are only halfway there. The bigger vision is not that we be atomized vessels sailing off in isolation, but a flotilla, working together to create a movement like Dunkirk.

Actually, this has always been the vision. We're tempted to focus only on our little Jerusalem. We struggle to contemplate neighboring Judea and Samaria, let alone the ends of the earth. However, the early church was interdependent. As the disciples scattered when persecution broke out at Stephen's martyrdom, they traveled to Phoenicia, Cyprus, and Antioch. Disciples from both Cyprus and Cyrene together went to Antioch to tell the good news to Greeks. When the church in Jerusalem heard about this, they sent Barnabas to encourage them. Barnabas tracked down Saul in Tarsus, and they settled in Antioch for a year. During that time, they raised financial aid to help the church in Judea before being set apart for their first missionary journey. These weren't isolated tribes. The early church was a broad movement of disciples functioning so evidently like a single body that they start to be collectively referred to as Christians (see Acts 11).

A bigger vision won't be created by new principles that need to be discovered but by old principles that need to be recovered, flowing from our faith in Jesus himself. What are the principles we find in the gospel itself that enlarge our vision?

Fidelity *IN CREASE OUR FAITH*

Our primary need is fidelity. Unless what we do is born out of and empowered by faith in Christ, we'll create a monster, not a movement. For those involved in gospel ministry, some of the most sobering words of Jesus were recorded by Matthew: "Many will say to me on that day, 'Lord, lord, did we not prophesy in your name and in your name drive out demons and in your name perform many miracles?' Then I will tell them plainly, 'I never knew you. Away from me, you evildoers!'" (Matthew 7:22-23).

We can be doers of prophecy, doers of exorcisms, and doers of miracles—*and also* be doers of evil. It isn't enough to preach, pastor, and plant; to evangelize, contextualize, and organize; to feed the poor, heal the sick, and house the homeless. In fact, "it requires far more than most people seem to think necessary, to save a soul."[10] (See again Acts 11.) It requires us to be rightly known by Jesus through repentance and faith, by his life-giving gospel. We begin there.

It's easy to lose sight of the Savior. I (John) learned this the hard way. For three years in a row, I picked up a mild illness from one of my kids, and rather than shaking it off, I was bedridden by it. I was exhausted for several weeks before I went to the doctor in search of a miracle cure. She heard my sorry tale and began to ask a few diagnostic questions.

"What do you do?" she enquired.

"I'm a church pastor," I replied.

She raised an eyebrow. "How many hours do you work on average?" I murmured a vague number.

She raised the other eyebrow. "When did you last take a day off?"

I squinted, as though trying to recall the date, looking up and hoping the ceiling tiles would provide me with an answer. "Erm," I began.

At this she rolled her eyes and put down her notebook. "John," she said, "just get some rest. You don't need to save the world today."

What a great evangelistic opportunity, I thought. *She doesn't realize that Jesus already is the savior of the world!* I was about to launch into my response when it hit me: She may not believe Jesus is the savior of the world—and *functionally*, with the way I was approaching ministry, neither did I.

When we take our eyes off Jesus, the danger is not just illness or burnout. We are on a trajectory that may end in moral failure, damage to the local church, and even apostasy. But when we begin with and remain in Jesus, that changes everything. As pastor and church-planting mentor Tim Keller wrote, "The gospel creates an entire way of life and affects literally everything about us."[11] The more deeply we reflect on Christ and his gospel, the more deeply he empowers us and the more richly the principles in this chapter are borne out in everything we do, including church planting.

Without faith in Christ, we are like cars with the wrong fuel in the engine. As we pull out of the gas station, we may not notice we absentmindedly put gas in a diesel tank; our car is still like every other car leaving the gas station. But twenty minutes into the journey, we come to a grinding halt.

Faith in Christ leads to a bigger vision. When we trust in ourselves, we only see small. The spiritual need we see is the one we think we can meet. The ministry opportunity we see is the one we think we can take. But when we trust in Christ, we begin to see big. It isn't about what we can do but about what he has done—and can do through us. Deep reflection on Christ, the gospel, and our world leads us to this conclusion: *The spiritual need and opportunity is far bigger than we think.*

Consider figure 1.1, "A bigger vision." Healthy mission-minded churches exist in box A. The Holy Spirit opens our eyes to see needs and opportunities that compel us to step out in evangelistic endeavors, train our members for witness, run group studies, have guest services, and create mission weeks.

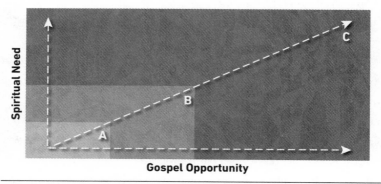

Figure 1.1. A bigger vision

For many churches, as they grow, so does their vision. At this point, they may move into box B. Here they consider planting churches or launching more services. They may also have an influence on a wider family of churches within their network or denomination.

However, both the spiritual need and the opportunity for mission is greater than we often realize. The gospel draws us into what we call a box-C vision, one that's too big for any single church, network, or denomination to pursue alone.

Box C is not new. It's the vision evangelicals have often embraced when it comes to reaching the nations. The heartbeat of global mission is the knowledge that because we have a world to reach, we must do it together. This realization is also at the heart of local collaborative church planting. But do we see it happening?

Many of the churches connected to 2020birmingham have been on a journey through the boxes. For example, one well-established church lived happily in box A. They faithfully engaged its community with the good news of Jesus. They grew steadily over the years and undertook a fantastic building project that's serving them well in their mission. They're in good fellowship with many other local churches, but they had a blind spot when it came to church planting—by their own admission.

They became aware of a church revitalization opportunity within their network. As they talked, they realized they were the church best placed to help. They entered box B but were feeling overwhelmed and started looking for help. They saw the need and the opportunity, but they couldn't be the solution on their own.

At that point, they began to talk with 2020birmingham. A collaborative effort, with them taking the lead, began to emerge. For the first time, they began to live in box C. Neil helped to recruit a family who may be able to lead the revitalization project, and John was involved in discussions with the church about preparing for revitalization. Churches within 2020birmingham considered whether there were people they could send to join the work. And within a relatively short space of time, it all came together.

The church may have stayed in box B and undertaken revitalization alone. However, it likely would have been a one-off project that would have required considerable recovery time. The project would have been weaker without access to a pool of resources, a growing body of local knowledge, and peer-to-peer support. This way, they skipped box B, entered box C, and are again actively looking for ways they can collaborate.

Are you ready to embrace a vision for your whole city? Box-C vision is not related to a church's size or circumstances. If ministry performance dictates the scope of a vision, 99.9 percent of us will remain in box A. A handful will limp our way into box B, but we will go no further. Box-C vision isn't linked to our success but to our Savior. Jesus sent out the seventy-two disciples, and they returned focused on their performance, saying, "Lord, even the demons submit to us in your name" (Luke 10:17). However, he directed their vision away from their success and onto him, saying, "Do not rejoice that the spirits submit to you, but rejoice that your names are written in heaven" (10:20). Box-C vision doesn't rest on competency but on Christ.

Seeing big in terms of need and opportunity sets us on a trajectory toward a different, bigger outcome. It has been said that what we build today either empowers or restricts us tomorrow.[12] When we've spent a lifetime in boxes A and B, it's hard to leave them. But if we dare to dream, our mindset shifts. So "our thinking, our skills, our relationships, our sense of what is possible and what it takes all grow on the journey to big."[13] We still start small, but by seeing big, under God, we may be surprised by what is possible.

A Spiritual Need That's Bigger Than You Think

A vision shaped by the gospel begins with faith in Christ. Let's look together at four implications of the gospel that grow out of the foundational principle of fidelity: urgency, compassion, generosity, and humility. As God cultivates them in our hearts, he sharpens our vision.

The principles of urgency and compassion open our eyes to a spiritual need that's bigger than we think. Spiritual need is the vertical axis on the figure 1.1. As our urgency and compassion grow, we begin to be led into a box-C vision. Let's take each principle in turn.

Urgency. Fidelity to Christ cultivates urgency for his mission. We want what he wants. Paul began his letter to the Romans by describing himself as a debtor "both to Greeks and non-Greeks, both to the wise and the foolish" (Romans 1:14). He was under a divine obligation to preach the gospel (1:1). Elsewhere he spoke of how he was compelled to discharge his duties. In fact, he said, "Woe to me if I do not preach the gospel!" (1 Corinthians 9:16-17). And so Paul was *eager* to preach

(Romans 1:15). Having received the gospel, he now *owed* this gospel to everyone and was urgently paying off his debt.

The pastor David Platt has very helpfully drawn out of Paul's letter to the Romans four reasons why fidelity creates urgency.

We must urgently share Christ with lost people, he writes, "1. Because their knowledge of God is only enough to damn them to hell forever."[14] "Although they knew God, they neither glorified him as God nor gave thanks to him, but their thinking became futile and their foolish hearts were darkened" (Romans 1:21).

"2. Because the gospel of God is powerful enough to save them for heaven."[15] "For I am not ashamed of the gospel, because it is the power of God that brings salvation to everyone who believes: first to the Jew, then to the Gentile" (1:16).

"3. Because the plan of God warrants the sacrifices of his people."[16] "How, then, can they call on the one they have not believed in? And how can they believe in the one of whom they have not heard? And how can they hear without someone preaching to them?" (10:14).

"4. Because the Son of God deserves the praises of all peoples."[17] "Through [Jesus] we received grace and apostleship to call all the Gentiles to the obedience that comes from faith for his name's sake" (1:5).

Platt concludes, "He's saying (really shouting) in the Book of Romans, 'I owe, we owe, Christ to the nations, so let's go and make him known! We must do this. This is not an option. This is an obligation.'"[18] If we believe in the lostness of the lost, and the glory of Christ, it will compel us to urgent action.

John Knox (1513–1572) was a minister who led the Protestant reformation in Scotland. During that time, Mary, the Catholic queen of Scotland, was reported to have said, "I fear the prayers of John Knox more than all the armies of England." Why was she afraid? Because of Knox's remarkable, urgent prayer: "Give me Scotland, or I die!" Can we say that the outcome of our own Bible reading is a godly ambition so bold and a vision so big? Does fidelity lead to urgency in our lives?

Compassion. Fidelity also leads us to a compassion that drives us to our knees. The more our hearts are broken, the more the vision grows. When Jesus entered Jerusalem, he wept over the city unwilling to recognize God's king, saying, "If you, even you, had only known on this day what would bring you peace" (Luke 19:42). When was the last time we thought about our cities in such terms as these? As Paul wrote, "I have great sorrow and unceasing anguish in my heart. For I could wish that I myself were cursed and cut off from Christ for the sake of my people" (Romans 9:2-3). Do we have such a compassion for *our* people? Do we cry out, "My neighbors, if you only knew Jesus, who brings true peace!"?

What is your burden for the people in your city? Why do we struggle to embrace a bigger vision? Could it be that too often our postal address is incidental to who we are and what we seek to do. Yet, the gospel surely doesn't allow us to think or live that way. It is good news to real people in real places. The gospel doesn't waft like a vapor to the ends of the earth; it is carried by heralds who take responsibility for every person at every coordinate along the way. A discarnate messiah cannot save, and a discarnate missiology cannot make disciples.

British author David Goodhart wrote recently on the divides we experience in the United Kingdom. His argument is that we are made up of two types of people: "anywhere" and "somewhere" people. "Anywheres" are highly educated and mobile, value autonomy, and comfortably surf social change. "Somewheres" are more rooted, valuing security and familiarity, and are more connected to a group identity.[19] There is a large, privileged minority (perhaps a quarter of the population) that has the ability to thrive and prosper *anywhere,* and an even larger group (perhaps half the population) that is more geographically rooted, people of *somewhere*. The rest of the population sits between these two poles.

For Goodhart, this insight helps to explain a number of contemporary political, economic, and social divisions we experience. He notes, "Getting on in Britain means getting out, shaking the Somewhere dust off one's boots and forming new bonds with one's fellow Anywheres."[20] As a result, the more highly educated, affluent, and socially mobile tend to disconnect from any particular sense of place, while among the less-educated white community "three in five Britons still live within twenty miles of where they lived when aged 14."[21] It's hard for Anywheres to have a passionate commitment to a place. It isn't their home, and the law of averages suggests they won't be there long.

This dynamic is also at play in the local church. In the United Kingdom, 62 percent of people who regularly attend church identify as middle class; only 38 percent identify as working class.[22] Eighty-one percent have a university degree, in contrast to 27 percent of the population as a whole.[23] If this is so, the church is full of Anywheres with an anywhere mindset.

A big vision for *somewhere*, a city or community, can't be borne out of an anywhere mindset. But our approach to church ministry often comes from just that. Sunday feels more like a classroom than a community. Sermon applications are influenced by our favorite preachers on YouTube rather than by the people who live next door. Methods of outreach are chosen because everyone is doing them, rather than because of the trial-and-error of experience. It isn't difficult to see that a denomination or network of anywhere churches can fail to be concerned for its local community. Chances are, we overlook the vast majority of our neighbors and therefore will never reach our cities for Christ.

Having a burden for somewhere overwhelms us. It opens our eyes to the scale of the task before us. What if we began to say our work is not done until every community in our city is served by a Bible-teaching church? Somewhere churches can't be elsewhere; so to reach many Somewheres, partnership is essential.

By the grace of God, City Church, Birmingham (the church Neil pastors), has planted one new autonomous church, one new Sunday site, and an outreach ministry in a predominantly Muslim area. God willing, this is the first step in seeing a church planted for Muslim-background believers. City Church has also played a significant role in two church revitalizations and a church plant. Beyond that, it has contributed in a variety of ways to the planting of other churches in the city.

City Church tends to attract Anywheres who arrive in the city. It seeks to encourage its people to think about what it means to be on mission *somewhere*. How should they pray for the city? How can they be good neighbors? How can they serve their community? How can they share Christ in their context? City Church also continually sends people out to resource church plants they could not plant themselves, as these Anywheres begin to put down roots. City Church is a case study in how fruitfulness can increase exponentially with collaboration.

The vast spiritual need that casts us to our knees in prayer demands a vision that no single church, network, or denomination can possibly realize on its own. If God is gracious to us, he will show us that we aren't supposed to realize it on our own. Urgency and compassion drive collaboration.

An Opportunity for Mission That's Bigger Than You Think

Fidelity to Christ fosters *urgency* and *compassion*. It opens our eyes to see that the spiritual need is far bigger than we think. However, a deeper appreciation of the gospel cultivates two further principles—*generosity* and *humility*—which help us see that the opportunity for mission is bigger than we think. This is the horizontal "gospel opportunity" axis in figure 1.1. As our generosity and humility grow, we are led into a box-C vision.

Generosity. Matthew 9:38 is a wonderful verse. As Jesus went through the towns and villages, proclaiming the good news of the kingdom and manifesting all its blessings, he was deeply moved by the crowds. He looked out at the vast numbers of lost people, harassed and helpless, like sheep without a shepherd, and he had compassion. Then he turned to his disciples, saying, "The harvest is plentiful but the workers are few. Ask the Lord of the harvest, therefore, to send out workers into his harvest field" (Matthew 9:37-38). WORKERS GO OUT, NOT GATHER TOGETHER

This passage speaks of the overwhelming urgency of our task while reminding us of the compassionate love of Christ. It calls for the response of harvesters while also reminding us to cry out to the Lord of the harvest. It lays out clearly for us the spiritual need in a way that should compel us to prayer, commissioning, and action. But it also speaks of the opportunity for mission. The key word is *plentiful.* We are prone to despondency and shortsightedness, but this verse opens our eyes to fields that are ripe for harvest (see also John 4:35).

However, there is a second 9:38, in Mark.[24] It's a verse you would struggle to use as a slogan for a mission conference. John came bounding up to Jesus, reporting, "We saw someone driving out demons in your name and we told him to stop, because he was not one of us." Jesus immediately rebuked him, saying, "Whoever is not against us is for us." When it comes to gospel ministry, the master is far more inclusive than his disciples.[25]

Mark placed this exchange in a section of his gospel in which we're clearly to associate discipleship with childlike behavior. In a culture where children had the lowest status of all, Jesus said, "Anyone who wants to be first must be the very last, and the servant of all" before taking a child in his arms and stating, "Whoever welcomes one of these little children in my name welcomes me; and whoever welcomes me does not welcome me but the one who sent me" (Mark 9:35, 37). Jesus' point comes into focus just a few verses later as he rebuked his disciples with the words "Truly I tell you, anyone who will not receive the kingdom of God like a little child will never enter it" (10:15).

The point is this: disciples of Jesus are to be like little children, gladly and humbly occupying a low standing, refusing to elevate themselves one above the other and living in complete dependence on him. Our human instinct is to seek ways to make ourselves better than others, belonging to the "in" crowd, labeling others as outside of the camp and "not one of us." We are to resist this with every sanctified impulse in our bodies. *WE WANT TO BE THE "IT" CHURCH OR THE "IN" PEOPLE*

Consider the former elder in the church where I (John) embarked on a revitalization project. He made it crystal clear that he would rather see the church die than be revitalized, because some of those involved were not quite on the same page as him theologically. Consider then the defensive and exclusivist feelings that I had when a church planter belonging to another network approached me and explained that they would like to launch their plant in the second floor of a pub just a short walk from where our church meets. Then consider the defensive and exclusivist feelings he and I both felt when another planter from a network outside the city made it clear that they too would like to begin a new plant locally. Then consider that our local district has a population of about twenty-five thousand people, and none of us had a monopoly on reaching them with the gospel.

In reflecting on these two 9:38s, David Shaw, a tutor in New Testament and Greek at Oak Hill College, imagined C. S. Lewis's creation, Screwtape, preaching on a demonic Mission Sunday with the aim of promoting a toxic tribalism:

As His subjects gather themselves to work in some area of the harvest field, let them think that only their methods are proper, or that their small corner of some field is really the whole. Let them acknowledge only their efforts as "strategic" . . . and let them pray, but only for their labors. That way, with only a little effort, they can pray for His glory, but all the while seek their own.[26]

That's a terrifying sentiment to read in print. But are we terrified by such a sentiment in our hearts?

In contrast, the deeper our grasp of the gospel, the greater our generosity toward others will be. J. C. Ryle, speaking on these verses, remarked, "Is our neighbor warring against Satan? Is he really trying to labor for Christ? This is the grand question. Better a thousand times that the work should be done by other hands than not done at all."[27]

Ministry truly done in the name of Jesus is ministry that belongs to Jesus. Will we really refuse to consider partnership on earth with people we expect to spend eternity with in heaven?

Humility. Jesus is not the only one who commands such a radical generosity of spirit toward other believers. Paul does too. In Philippians 1, we see that generosity is underpinned with a remarkable gospel-wrought humility.

It is true that some preach Christ out of envy and rivalry, but others out of goodwill. The latter do so out of love, knowing that I am put here for the defense of the gospel. The former preach Christ out of selfish ambition, not sincerely, supposing that they can stir up trouble for me while I am in chains. But what does it matter? The important thing is that in every way, whether from false motives or true, Christ is preached. And because of this I rejoice. (Philippians 1:15-18)

Notice that fidelity to Christ is paramount. Paul maintained that where the true gospel is preached, there is reason to rejoice, even if the result is personal loss. Elsewhere Paul spoke out in the strongest terms against those whose preaching demonstrated that they were enemies of the gospel (for example, Galatians 1:6-10 and 1 Timothy 1:3-4). But here Paul was generous because his opponents were preaching the same gospel. Despite the envy and rivalry demonstrated by those who opposed him in Rome, they weren't preaching another gospel. Rather "these rivals to Paul instead seem to oppose the apostle for personal reasons and to have used Paul's imprisonment as an opportunity to advance their personal agendas."[28] It's not clear how they were seeking to stir up trouble. Markus Bockmuehl offers the most persuasive explanation when he suggests that they "stir up trouble by causing an inner turmoil and pain in Paul as they pursue naked self-advancement, numerical success, prestige and influence within the Roman church."[29] While Paul was in prison, they were free to promote their prideful position in the Christian community. Even though Paul may have struggled to endorse them and their methodology, he rejoiced because the gospel was preached.

Healthy church-planting movements depend upon developing a culture in which we choose to rejoice in the ministry success of others. I hope our relationships with other churches would not be defined as ones of envy and rivalry. How much more should we also rejoice that the gospel is preached beyond our tribe.

I (John) described above the exclusivist feelings that so quickly arise when we feel the threat of very different churches launching around us. It has been a challenge not to become defensive and instead to see how we can help. We've had to ask ourselves, do we love this city enough and are we kingdom-minded enough to be just as excited at witnessing revival break out in the church meeting in the pub down the road as we would be to see it happen with us?

In a collaborative movement, this happens a lot. A church leader gives time and effort to a bigger vision and as a consequence a network or denomination he is not personally affiliated to benefits. It may advance ahead of him and his tribe. Collaborating in such instances requires great humility.

For Paul, furthering the gospel was everything, and self-interest gave way to God's concern. "The important thing is that in every way, whether from false motive or true, Christ is preached" (Philippians 1:18). Paul certainly did care about the motives of those who preach the gospel (see for example, 1 Corinthians 13 and 1 Timothy 4:16). But that wasn't his point. He was clear here: the gospel must advance, whatever the cost to him.

Pastor and theologian Gordon Fee wrote, "In Paul's case it is his theological convictions that lead both to his theological narrowness, on the one hand, and to his large-heartedness within those convictions, on the other—precisely because he recognizes the gospel for what it is: God's thing, not his own."[30] Sadly such humility is often lacking, even when the charges are far less serious. To quote Professor Frank Thielman, "The fellowship of the modern church lies in tatters because of rivalry over turf, competition for money and influence, and petty theological disagreements."[31]

For Paul, fidelity to Christ meant there were reasons to rejoice in the advancement of the gospel amid insincerity, false motive, and personal heartache. *How much more* should faithful churches be willing to extend generosity and act with humility toward those who are willing to be partners with us?

A Cautionary Tale

John the church planter leaned over the bridge railing and gazed down into the water below. The core team meeting hadn't gone as planned. The caretaker had been late opening up, the new couple never showed up, the feedback from Sunday felt particularly personal, and for some reason the prepared handouts had printed back to front again. And this after only Doris had shown for the family outreach event, with Bobby, her Jack Russell, who had quietly devoured all the sausage rolls. *This isn't working.* John thought, staring into the abyss below. *Would anyone notice if we stopped? And would anyone notice if I just quietly disappeared?*

At just that moment, Neil walked onto the bridge. "Hi there. You're looking kind of down," he said in his characteristic melodic timbre. "Do you want to talk? You know life's never without hope!"

"I know," confessed John reluctantly. "I'm a Christian actually."

"That's amazing," Neil said, stepping nearer. "I'm a Christian too."

"Yeah? I'm actually a church planter, though we are kind of struggling at the moment."

"I'm a church planter too. Church of England, or Independent?"

"Independent," confessed John.

"Me too!" Neil replied even more excitedly. "Baptist or Congregational?"

"Congregational."

"Me too! Continuationist or Cessationist?"

"Continuationist."

"Me too! ESV or NIV?"

"NIV."

"Me too! Missional communities or home groups?"

"Home groups."

"Die heretic!" Neil cried, and he pushed John off the bridge.[32]

That conversation could have been very different. If judgment were replaced with encouragement, we wouldn't push potential ministry partners off the bridge. Yet we often use fidelity as the reason to pass over cooperation with other churches. In order to withdraw, we say, "To be faithful, we must remain pure." <u>We argue that orthodoxy requires isolation, but the opposite is true.</u> Fidelity causes us to be concerned about guarding the gospel, but it also compels us to go with the gospel. This requires compassion, generosity, and humility, all of which cause us to acknowledge we simply cannot and should not attempt to spread the gospel on our own.

Only a deeper grasp of the gospel will open our eyes to see that both the spiritual need and the opportunity for mission are far bigger than we think. These two propel us into a box-C vision, where we grasp the need for collaboration.

As dependent children corporately clinging to Christ, we must learn that the only "us and them" that matters in eternity is not a division within the kingdom of God but *us* who have been found pursuing *them*, his lost sheep. As we answer the call and live for this mission, we should build bridges not barricades and throw ropes not rocks.

A Spreading Vision

2020birmingham is what God has begun to make possible in our city. And around the world there is a growing recognition that the gospel compels us toward collaboration. In 2017 church leaders from twenty-seven major cities across Europe met to consider how collaborative church-planting movements can be nurtured. In the United States, conversations are taking place in New York, Austin, Baltimore, Chicago, Miami, and Washington, DC.[33] Later in this book, we'll include contributions from Hamburg in Germany, Tokyo in Japan, Pretoria in South Africa, Chicago in the United States, and Valparaiso in Chile—that is, stories from Europe, Asia, Africa, North America, and South America.

Many of these fledgling movements have been helped by the ministry of Redeemer City to City, the City to City network, and various related networks. In fact, the inspiration, encouragement, and support of City to City has been key to the progress 2020birmingham has made. City to City's vision is to see new movements of the gospel in every major city of the world.

It may be helpful to view City to City as an attempt to bridge the gap between global Anywheres and local Somewheres—a global network of local collaborative movements that could not exist just anywhere but instead are shaped by the context and the people they long to reach. For these groups to flourish into movements, important *anywhere* connections will be needed, but they can't be the whole answer. *Somewhere* connections will be key: connections between neighbors motivated by urgency, compassion, generosity, and humility.

Your community exists *somewhere* and needs a *somewhere* movement. What might God do if churches all over the world began to see that they need this bigger vision to reach their locality for Christ?

Beginnings

All through history
God has chosen and used nobodies.

OSWALD CHAMBERS

In this chapter we'll introduce you to 2020birmingham. First we'll retell the story of its conception and birth then explain how we have sought to cultivate increasing unity, diversity, multiplication, and depth as a fledgling movement. Then we'll raise the question of what it may mean for you to embark on a journey like this in your own context.

A Cup of Coffee and a Bigger Vision

Like many good stories, this one begins with a cup of coffee. In fact, it begins with two cups of coffee some five years apart. The first was in the spring of 2004 at the Evangelical Ministry Assembly in London when I (Neil) met with Al Barth from the Redeemer

Church Planting Center (now called City to City) in New York. Our church was four years old, and I told him I was an "accidental and reluctant" church planter. Despite this, Al asked if he could visit. He arrived in September for our fifth-anniversary service. Perfect timing!

Over the next four years, Al and the team at City to City began to share the vision they had for the cities of the world, and so a bigger vision for *my* city began to form in me. This was something of a conversion moment, as I began to make the journey from box A all the way to box C in my thinking. I then traveled to a church-planting conference in New York and began to see how a local collaborative church-planting movement may emerge back in Birmingham. In other words, without Al, this book would never have been written. City to City gave me the tools to make this vision a reality.

In 2009 I attended a discussion of church planting with the Midlands Gospel Partnership, a regional coalition of conservative evangelical churches. We were all like-minded, white, and middle class. We talked about the spiritual needs of Birmingham, but it was clear that none of the churches represented in the room had any intention of planting within the next five years. This was another conversion moment for me. I had already been persuaded of a box-C vision, but that meeting was the catalyst I needed to begin to gather a wider coalition of churches to partner at a different level to meet the need of my city.

I realized that if we were going to make an impact for Christ in Birmingham, a city of more than a million people, I needed to start talking to churches I had never talked to before. I knew there must be churches in our city that shared this bigger vision and may be willing to collaborate, though we may not share the same doctrinal distinctives and may look culturally different on the ground.

A Cup of Coffee and a New Friendship

So, in 2009 I had my second significant cup of coffee. I asked another local pastor, Jonathan Bell, if he would consider a conversation about working together for the good of our city.

We had never met before or visited one another's churches. I knew that he was an established church planter working with New Frontiers in the city, but it had not crossed our minds that we might partner in ministry. Our circles were very different. I came to faith, was mentored, and ministered in a theologically conservative context with a strong emphasis on Scripture and not much emphasis at all on the Holy Spirit. I had planted reluctantly and out of necessity in the city where I'd grown up.

My impression of Jonathan was that he was a man on a clear mission from God to reach the city for Jesus. He and his wife had come to Birmingham with that sole purpose, and he was confidently and joyfully accomplishing what he had been called to do (or so it appeared to me). The family of churches he belonged to had emerged precisely because of a conviction that there was a lack of emphasis on the Holy Spirit in the church in the United Kingdom.

So we belonged to different tribes not by accident but out of conviction. We knew different people, we read different books, we went to different conferences, we probably liked different types of coffee.

Yet we had both planted churches that had planted churches in the same city, so we had at least that in common. What we discovered was that we had the same love of the Lord Jesus, the same vision to see the whole city renewed by the gospel, the same conviction that church planting was central to that task, and the same understanding that the job was bigger than either of us alone. We also discovered we could be friends.

Jonathan had been traveling on his own journey into box C and had his own conversion moments toward a bigger vision. He reflected,

When I moved to Birmingham to church plant back in 1996, I thought we were the answer. Everyone else in the city who'd been faithfully laboring for years and years clearly weren't doing it right. What the city desperately needed was for us to plant "a proper church" that would somehow spread through the whole city and put right what all the other churches were doing wrong! Thirteen years in, we'd flogged our guts out planting a further six churches in the greater Birmingham area—but it still felt like a drop in the ocean.

At the point that Neil contacted me, I was beginning to wake up to the fact that the scale of the need in the city required working more intentionally with others than I'd previously been prepared for. More than that, I was coming to see that my need for others was significantly greater than their need for me. Looking back, if God hadn't graciously challenged my pride and sense of independence prior to meeting up with Neil, we probably would have ended up throwing coffee over each other! As it was, God had clearly been preparing the ground in both of us so that the seed of an idea quickly took root and grew in ways neither of us could have dared to believe would be possible.

Having been persuaded intellectually and prompted to take action, I was becoming convinced this might actually work. This was the third conversion moment. I was beginning to turn from an accidental and reluctant church planter into someone who desired to do all he could to see as many churches as possible planted across our city and to the glory of God. And I wasn't alone. The boundary had been crossed, and however important our distinctives were to Jonathan and me, what we had in common was far greater. What began as a coffee conversation became a partnership that would see us commit to working together for ten years with the aim of helping to plant twenty new churches.

Getting Started

2020birmingham was launched in 2010. The very name was our attempt to put our goal as an aspiring movement "up front and center." Twenty new congregations in a ten-year window was certainly a stretch goal but a credible one as well. Having a target is quite un-British, but it has kept us focused. "What number are you up to?" is a question we have to answer all the time. It has helped us spread the vision. It has helped us raise money. It has helped us celebrate milestones.

Collaborative partnership isn't necessarily helped by inviting everyone to be part of it from the start. So we launched with a low-key conference; we didn't rent a stadium or an auditorium. Small but strong was key to providing a solid foundation of relationships on which to build.

As we launched, we sought to embody the principles of fidelity, urgency, compassion, generosity, and humility outlined in the previous chapter. We may not have articulated things very clearly back then, but as we cast the vision, we renewed our faith in Christ, considered the urgency of the task, and focused on the call to be compassionate.

We also sought to demonstrate a generosity of spirit. We invited the Anglican bishop of Aston (a Church of England bishop in the city of Birmingham and an experienced church planter himself) to address the conference. As two church planters at home in nonconformity, Jonathan and I reaching out to the Church of England was a statement of intent regarding who we were willing to learn from and work alongside. We also attempted to draw in others, including the well-established Birmingham City Mission. Looking for partnership set a tone of weakness rather than strength. That wasn't difficult, since none of us knew what we were doing—or where it would lead.

That September, John returned from Bible college to begin a revitalization project, the first 2020birmingham church plant. Church revitalization is not quite a replant, in which a church closes and is replanted as something entirely new. It's a process of deliberate change undertaken by the church family with new leadership and usually with people added from outside to get things going. The church in question had been planted seventy-five years previously but was almost at the point of closure. John and Sarah returned to the city, connected with 2020birmingham, and embarked on the project.

Forming Unity

We focused on relationships. Our first big priority was to establish the planters forum, our monthly meeting for planters that includes peer-to-peer prayer, support, training, and informal coaching. The atmosphere we try to foster is one of honesty and accountability. Our prayer is that it has a culture where we can share our successes and also find grace in our time of need.

We meet for around two and a half hours. We tell stories, pray for one another, and finish by eating together. Planters feel they have permission to share fears and concerns alongside hopes and dreams. It's a place where people own their mistakes and ask for help. On more than one occasion, a planter has been honest enough to say he felt like giving up.

In the early days of the planters meeting together, there were just four or five of us. Occasionally we even canceled meetings because of

A TYPICAL PLANTERS FORUM

10:00–10:30	Arrive for coffee and donuts
10:30–11:15	Tell stories and celebrate the wins
11:15–11:30	Pray for one another in small groups
11:30–11:40	Break for more coffee
11:40–12:30	Peer-to-peer training session
12:30	Lunch and networking

a lack of numbers. God has given the growth, and now we sometimes have more than twenty at our monthly meetings. And we look back on the early days knowing that was the way to grow sustainably.

The "Planters Forum Syllabus 2010" sidebar, from the first year, lists the subjects we tackled. The syllabus was planned and taught by the experienced planters in the group, with others occasionally leading sessions that were pertinent to them. We resisted the temptation to bring in outside experts, preferring that we could all have a voice and grow in our understanding together. Each year the content was refreshed, the range of topics expanded, and the fundamentals reinforced. Alongside the following sessions, we had case studies on church plants across the city.

PLANTERS FORUM SYLLABUS 2010 (YEAR 1)

- Your Context
- Setting Out Vision and Core Values
- Building a Missional Community and Using Community Service to Share Christ
- Building and Developing a Powerful Team—Raising Leaders
- Establishing Personal Ministry Patterns and Priorities (New Resolutions for a New Year!)
- Supporting the Weak within the Congregation
- Loving the Unlovely and Supporting the Difficult—Pastoring Sinners for Change
- Identifying and Utilizing the Gifts of the Church and Lessons Learned
- Preaching to the Unbeliever and Believer in a TV-Oriented Culture
- Nurturing the Church's Prayer Life and Battling in a Spiritual War

- ▣ Social Action and Serving the Community
- ▣ Practicalities and Responsibilities of Running a Church Plant
- ▣ Money and Budget Setting
- ▣ Multiculturalism and Different Models of Church Plants: From Heterogeneous to Homogeneous
- ▣ Relating to Other Churches and Organizations
- ▣ Book Review—*Life Together* by Dietrich Bonhoeffer

2020birmingham has never had a strategic plan for how or where we would find twenty church planters or plant twenty new congregations, so we weren't sure what we were trying to build. But we were sure about our DNA. It was a step of faith. Later in the book, we'll detail the formula we've been using for collaboration and the vital role the DNA code plays in that. At this point, it's important to note that 2020birmingham didn't begin by starting a program but by cherishing and celebrating the gospel-wrought dynamics and values at the heart of our relationships.

Our clear stretch goal generated some interest among local leaders and so did the unity that was on display between churches that were quite different from each other. They were asking, "How are such different churches able to collaborate in a meaningful partnership?" This not only raised interest but also gave 2020birmingham credibility. Something was going on that was worth considering.

Early on, we saw churches established by a number of pioneer church planters who had moved into the city and gathered core teams. These planters had wider partnerships that helped them get established, but it was telling that they also chose to connect quickly to 2020birmingham as a natural local context for peer-to-peer support. It offered a unique kind of collaboration, adding value at a local level to what they were already seeking to do.

Developing Diversity

A couple of years in, we named our annual conference "How to Win a Million." It focused on the size and urgency of the task to reach every community in the city for Jesus. It was an attempt to recognize the cultural diversity of Birmingham while acknowledging how white and middle class the churches that made up 2020birmingham were. To try to connect more widely, we invited speakers to help us address this concern, and we held a networking meal for leaders of black-majority churches in the city.

That year we saw Daniel and Elena Bara move to the city and pioneer the Romanian-speaking Emmaus Church. Daniel had previously led three churches in Romania but had a call to plant churches in the United Kingdom. After having a vision of a map of the city of Birmingham, he got in touch with Neil, having found 2020birmingham online. The presence of 2020birmingham gave him the ability to connect quickly with others working locally. The same year Abraham Belew, a member of City Church, planted the Ethiopian Evangelical Church in the city. Although there remained much to do, God was beginning to answer our prayer for cultural diversity.

Since the onset, when we set our ambitious goals, our conviction to see churches planted across our city has only grown. We see it as our problem that there are so many unreached communities around us. It has become our goal to do what we can to help reach the least-reached people groups in Birmingham, most of whom come from countries closed to the gospel or with no church in their own tongue. For these first-generation immigrants, there is an opportunity and a need. Without wanting to disclose sensitive details, we can say that God is beginning to raise up workers among them.

We've taken risks with who we're willing to work with. The risks are measured and prayed over, but to reach a city we must collaborate with leaders and churches we've never considered working with before. For a task so great, such a level of risk seems right. And out of those risks has come great reward.

As you think about future partnership, do you wonder if there is anyone who shares your vision for what could happen in your city?

Multiplying

We saw God at work, and we worked with him. God is giving the growth as we plant and water. We had no idea where our planters would come from or how it would happen, and God has been full of surprises. He has raised up planters in unexpected ways and from unexpected places.

A significant proportion of our plants have happened because people contacted us and asked if they may partner. This reinforces the importance of having a localized collaborative movement alongside other networks and denominations. For example, that surprising phone call from a church pastor in Romania led him to join us a few months later. An Ethiopian taxi driver who had come to the United Kingdom for theological training found his way to Neil's church and then into planting. A Mexican asylum seeker, wonderfully converted, was keen to reach out to his fellow Spanish speakers. None of these individuals were known to us, but we worked where God was at work. We have seen seventeen churches planted, which is a testimony to the fact that God has been the one at work in and through this unlikely collective.

As things have gotten going, we've begun to spread the word. We were happy to have started small, but we've since worked hard to get the message out to the wider church. We knew that having a long-term impact on our city for Christ and truly becoming a movement would require a change of culture across the churches in our city. Many more churches needed to grasp a vision for planting. Our goal, you could say, is not just to plant twenty new churches that would in turn plant new churches; rather it is to see every faithful church in our city ask, "What can we do to play our part?"

Part of our strategy to achieve this has been an annual conference where we tell stories of what God is doing through church planting in the city to envision a wider community of church leaders. Typically thirty to thirty-five churches now attend the annual event, and nine conferences later, we can see that some churches have become church-planting churches.

We're rarely a planter's primary network; many planters already have their own coaching relationships and support structures. This has added to our diversity and aided our multiplication, because 2020birmingham has worked best when it's working alongside national and international networks. Functioning as the secondary network is inevitably complex, because each planter has differing needs, and there is no benefit in unnecessary duplication. So, for example, in most cases we haven't assessed planters but have accepted the assessment provided by their own planting network.

Planters gain the benefits of input from their denomination or network but also get all the benefits of a city movement, particularly in the form of local collaboration, shared knowledge, and peer-to-peer support. We can fill in the gaps where needed; but more importantly, we offer the unique strength of being wholeheartedly dedicated to reaching our city.

What 2020birmingham is able to provide for everyone is a forum where we can work out what it practically means for us to be together for our city. Put another way, a primary network may offer a series of strong and important relational ties, but it's unlikely to share a united concern for a single city and has little or no scope for multiplication at a local level. A secondary network like 2020birmingham may offer weaker ties initially, but those ties may be just the connections that kick-start the kind of citywide movement that will accomplish more together than is possible alone.

Historian Niall Ferguson has written about viral networks (what we call "movements" in this book), observing, "Weak ties . . . are the vital bridges between disparate clusters that would otherwise not be connected at all." He goes on to conclude, "Put simply, the greater number of nodes in a network, the more valuable the network to the nodes collectively. . . . This implies spectacular returns to very large, open-access networks and, conversely, limited returns to secret and/or exclusive networks."[1]

2020birmingham is, in Ferguson's language, an open-access network of both strong and weak ties in the hope that church planting may go viral in our city. This is what we mean when we describe it as a localized, collaborative church-planting movement.

Going Deeper

At certain points over the past eight years, we've sought to think about what it means for us to make a deep impact on our cities through church planting. The vision is not just to plant some new churches but to begin a gospel movement that will seek to serve and bless the city even as it holds out the word of life. Church planting is the core and key catalyst for this to happen. As part of the annual conference, we've invited speakers to help us to engage with the city through social action, the arts, and politics. To try to understand our city better, we invited the Birmingham City Council to speak to us on some of the challenges and opportunities they face. We have also run seminars on what it means for us to attempt to reach Pakistani Muslims, Eastern Europeans, and post-Christian secular people in our city.

People who have a desire to plant churches among the least-reached people groups in our city have also connected with us. We recently saw our seventeenth work take shape. Without supplying specific details, this is a small community center run by Christians in a hard-to-reach part of the city. The center managers, in partnership with their mission agency and 2020birmingham, have a vision to see it as a training platform in crosscultural inner-city ministry, while itself being the first step in seeing a church planted there.

This has been a season of waking up to the need to invest in our organization's infrastructure to ensure further growth. By the grace of God, we haven't seen a church plant established in partnership with 2020birmingham fail, but we recognize the importance not just of numerical growth but also of health. To see a self-sustaining movement requires us to work for healthy churches that will multiply. Recently we've sought to strengthen the organizational support around the movement, such as by having a training workshop on "gospel coaching" with Scott Thomas, the US Director for C2C Network, to help us introduce a more rigorous coaching strategy. We also began to employ Andy Weatherley as a movement trainer one day a week; he has developed the delivery of City to City's Incubator, a sixteen-module training program to resource church planters as they prepare to plant or have just planted. Andy is an experienced church planter who has been a part of 2020birmingham from its conception. We also launched a prayer campaign, recognizing that this was a key part of the life of the movement and a way people can partner in an effective way. Finally, 2020birmingham took part in the City to City European Network Leaders Forum in Rome as well as a global network leaders forum at City to City, New York. These were great ways to connect with other movement leaders in other cities around the world.

We were invited to Alabama to begin a Birmingham-to-Birmingham mission partnership with Briarwood Presbyterian Church, which has developed into a long-standing commitment to support church planting in our city. SaRang Church in Seoul invited us to South Korea to strengthen a relationship as they seek to support church planting and revitalization across Europe.

Revisiting the Vision

To reach a city requires a self-sustaining movement of church-planting churches. In other words twenty churches has to be just the beginning. Twenty churches by 2020 was our original aspiration, but now we would love to see another thirty by 2030. To see that happen, we need to raise up a whole new generation of people who understand the need and are equipped to play their part.

Our theme in 2018 has been the next generation, and our aim is to identify, equip, and send out the next generation of workers into the mission field. We launched a series of Next Generation vision evenings for those with leadership potential to help them understand the DNA of 2020birmingham. One key development this year has been the launch of Parakaleo,[2] a context where planters' spouses can find support.

With a number of exciting projects being planned by churches within the movement, we are trusting God for the final three church plants needed to reach our goal. If each of these plants has planting others in its DNA, we pray we may see true multiplication in our lifetime—more than one hundred new or revitalized churches in our generation—and the city renewed by the gospel.

Much has happened over the past ten years, and there is much we are praying for. One thing is certain: those two cups of coffee were probably the best I ever drank.

As you think about your own context, ask what it may mean for you to step beyond your primary network into something bigger. If Niall Ferguson is right, "weak ties are strong."[3] You can do more together than you can on your own, and your city needs you to reach out across the old boundary lines. Who knows where a cup of coffee may take you?

Movements

You can't stay in your corner of the forest waiting for others to come to you. You have to go to them sometimes.

WINNIE-THE-POOH

In this chapter, we'll cover the following:

- *what collaborative church-planting movements are;*
- *why they offer a unique opportunity for partnership across traditional boundaries;*
- *what the dynamics of healthy spiritual movements are;*
- *why movements offer a distinctive context for pursuing collaboration and localism; and*
- *how a movement is different from a network or a denomination, and why we need them all.*

In the summer of 2014, people began to post social media videos of themselves having buckets of water poured over their heads. They either invited someone to do it to them or happily administered the bucketful themselves. From their gasps and shrieks, it was clear the water was freezing cold. Why were they doing this? For the Ice Bucket Challenge, which raised awareness and funds for research of amyotrophic lateral sclerosis, a motor neuron disease. Victims nominated their friends, who in turn nominated their friends, and a *movement* was born.

Or was it?

Last year my (John's) children returned from school after spending much of the day frozen in action while a camera moved among them and a clean version of "Black Beatles" by Rae Sremmurd played in the background. When I asked what this had to do with their multiplication tables, I was educated on the Mannequin Challenge. Although its origin is unknown, it spread quickly and involved notable participants, including Michelle Obama, Bill Gates, and Naomi Campbell. A movement was born.

Or was it?

Both were viral trends: short-lived enthusiasm for fashionable novelties often detached from their original meaning and forgotten as quickly as they began. This raises an important point: true movements are by nature difficult to define. Because of this, Alan Hirsch, a thought leader in the missional church movement, wrote *"Movements are felt as much as they are understood. They have a certain atmosphere. They exude a culture, and people sense the resulting 'vibe.' These vibes cannot be objectively passed along and studied. They must be caught and experienced."*[1]

We live in a cultural moment when—to adapt Ecclesiastes 12:12—of making many movements there is no end. They are many and varied, and if we aren't careful, we are in danger of experiencing movement fatigue. The purpose of this chapter is to define carefully what we mean by a movement and to identify what we believe constitutes healthy movement dynamics of the kind we're advocating in this book.

What Makes a Movement?

Movements have a life of their own. They have an internal vitality. According to Tim Keller, "A church (or group of churches) with movement dynamics generates its own converts, ideas, leaders, and resources from within in order to realize its vision of being the church for its city and culture."[2] At the heart of any movement is *self-sustaining growth*. This is intrinsic to the word *movement* itself, which suggests life, action, change, direction, and progress.

This vitality is generated because, first and foremost, movements grow out of a vision. People are drawn together and energized by shared convictions of what the future could or should look like and how that change can happen. For example, the conviction that workers' rights ought to be protected gave rise to the Labour movement in the United Kingdom. That movement is a collective united by a clearly defined goal. In the same way, the Occupy movement was born in reaction to a perceived lack of democracy and increasing inequality.

For a movement to begin, seemingly disparate groups unite around a shared set of convictions that things must change, which then energizes all they do together. This primary feature of movements is so important that chapter one was dedicated to the five foundational principles that create box-C vision. Later in the book, we'll seek to understand how those principles are then contextualized into a DNA code that energizes a collaborative church-planting movement.

Though all movements share the core characteristics of *vitality* and *vision*, not all are alike. Some are built around deferring to a charismatic leader to whom all participants feel an affinity, such as Martin Luther King Jr. and the civil rights movement in America. Others are grassroots and nonhierarchical, such as church-planting movements in modern-day China. Some grow within the existing structures of an institution with no desire to partner more widely, while others regard some form of cross-party collaboration as fundamental to their progress. Some are highly organized and propagate by utilizing the latest technology; others are entirely organic and deliberately resist a formal strategic plan.

It's tempting to pit competing definitions against one another and to draw up a list of qualities that separate "good" and "bad" movements. But there are complex reasons why any movement develops in the way it does. So we'll suggest a collection of key dynamics that bring a certain health to our kind of movement—one born out of and shaped by the gospel. This isn't an arbitrary quality; the more a collaborative church-planting movement is defined by the gospel, the healthier it will be, and with health will come a certain attractiveness, usefulness, and—by God's grace—fruitfulness. The kind of movements our cities need depend on a deep understanding of the gospel, and this glorious gospel creates these healthy dynamics.[3]

Open membership. In 2020birmingham we don't have a list of responsibilities that are prerequisites for belonging to the group. Instead we have a committed core of churches willing to give whatever it takes to advance the planting of churches across the city. They ask for nothing in return, and they claim no glory for themselves; rather, they delight in the fact that Jesus is increasingly being made known in needy communities. We also have a fringe of people that are simply welcome to come and see, welcome to receive anything of value, welcome to add their voice, and welcome to play their part.

According to Keller, a key difference between movements and institutions is that movements retain a generous flexibility toward those outside their membership rolls. As a result, "members of a movement are willing to make allies, cooperating with anyone who shares an interest in the vision."[4] In part two, we'll discuss the difference between open and closed membership and what collaboration across tribal boundaries can look like in practice. At this point it's important to recognize that an open membership and what we will later explore as a "center set" approach to collaboration is driven primarily by this dynamic of generosity.

Movements recognize that their vision is caught and not simply taught; people are welcome to come and see and receive without having to prove they're fully onboard. Movements are marked by freely giving and receiving time and resources. Strikingly, as members catch the vision and begin to share the core values of the movement, they're drawn to the center, and they begin to display a remarkably generous servant-heartedness. A movement is not simply a resource or equipping center, and "if the top leaders . . . are the only ones making all the sacrifices, then you don't have a movement culture."[5] Members of a healthy movement learn quickly that it's better to give than to receive.

It shouldn't be difficult to see how a grasp of the gospel creates this kind of generosity toward nonmembers. At the heart of the gospel is the idea that everything we have, we have received from God as a free and undeserved gift. Becoming givers extends way beyond personal evangelism. Why should we not willingly and actively seek to give away our time and energy—and our money too—to equip other churches for mission? Paul didn't need to command the church in Corinth to give generously to bless other churches. He simply reminded them of "the grace of our Lord Jesus Christ, that though he was rich, yet for your sake he became poor, so that you through his poverty might become rich" (2 Corinthians 8:9). As one author noted,

"Some Christians give according to their means; and some Christians give according to their meanness!"[6] When we look as Jesus himself, we know movements should excel in the grace of giving.

Spontaneity and organic organization. Another typical feature of this type of movement is a preference for spontaneity over strategic planning, especially in the early stages. Church-planting movements are best generated by a shared culture, not a strict process. They emerge not because of big-box programming but through small, readily reproducible units.[7] They have no "prescribed formula . . . for how or where these churches will exist or function."[8]

2020birmingham has never really had a plan. We had a vision to see twenty new churches but no clear idea as to where they would come from. We made things up as we went along. This lack of premeditation works to bring about interesting innovations, accidental successes, and fruitfulness from unexpected quarters. Unlikely partnerships, serendipitous discoveries, and unforeseen advances emerge.

If, as we outlined above, the essence of a movement is an internal vitality and vision, then movements, like all living things, have the capacity to grow from the inside out. A lack of external influence produces new ideas and leaders from within and empowers ordinary people to play their part in something bigger with an apparent life of its own. A spontaneous and organic movement is "self-propagating, self-governing, and self-supporting."[9] It takes responsibility for generating whatever it needs to realize its vision.

At times, it feels as though 2020birmingham has developed *despite* us, with a life and energy all of its own. There is no global plan, no governing patron, and no Grand Poobah. Instead there is an internal vitality and vision that brings surprising results. We've simply sought to take responsibility for developing what's needed to be a movement for our city at this time, but this has often happened reactively. We've sought to forge friendships wherever possible and have found our-selves responding to opportunities that presented themselves.

Three wonderful examples of this are emerging right now. We have often prayed as a group for God to raise up the right planters for the hardest-to-reach areas of our city, particularly those districts that are overwhelmingly Muslim and where the church is in rapid decline. Although we can't publish details relating to those three projects, as God has raised up the workers, 2020birmingham has been in the right space for churches to gather, hear of the need, and begin to respond to what God is doing.

In the first instance, we've sought to raise up planters and create opportunities to plant from within the movement itself. As the movement has grown, new players, won by the vision, have increased the scope for spontaneity.

Theologian and missiologist Lesslie Newbigin captured something of this when he wrote about the "logic of mission":

> There has been a long tradition which sees the mission of the Church primarily as obedience to a command. It has been cus-tomary to speak of "the missionary mandate." This way of putting the matter is certainly not without justification, and yet it seems to me that it misses the point. It tends to make mission a burden rather than a joy, to make it part of the law rather than part of the gospel. If one looks at the New Testament evidence one gets another impression. *Mission begins with a kind of ex-plosion of joy.* The news that the rejected and crucified Jesus is alive is something that cannot possibly be suppressed. It must be told. Who could be silent about such a fact? The mission of the Church in the pages of the New Testament is more like the fallout from a vast explosion, a radioactive fallout which is not lethal but life-giving.[10]

Leadership by influence. The story is told of a group of British pastors on a trip to Israel. Their tour guide explains that the shepherds there don't walk behind the sheep, driving them, but rather walk in front, leading them as they follow, just as they did in Jesus' time. At that moment, they look out of the coach window to see a man walking behind his flock, driving them along with a stick. "I thought you said the shepherds here always lead the sheep," said one of the group. "They do," replied the guide. "This man isn't the shepherd. He's the butcher."

In the kind of movement we're advocating, there's an absence of a hierarchy or a command chain. Leadership is exercised through the influence of peers rather than through the voice of an appointed authority. Leaders with an ability to catalyze growth emerge as they provide vision and inspiration within the movement. The general rule is to structure just as much as is necessary to adequately empower every partner to do his or her job.[11] Movements are therefore nervous about the negative effect of institutionalization, such as a resistance to change and a suspicion of outsiders. As Hirsch notes, we must "resist the tendency, innate to every organization, to slow down and lose momentum."[12] Spiritual movements are by their nature bottom-up rather than top-down. Outside of the boundaries of an established network or denomination, what emerges is necessarily grassroots, proliferating within and across networks of relationships.[13]

That is precisely how 2020birmingham began: as a network of relationships. There are no appointed directors of the movement. The leadership that exists has emerged only to meet the needs of the movement. The DNA is indeed protected by these leaders, but also by the group, galvanized by the unifying vision. We have charitable trustees and Andy Weatherley, recently appointed director of training (a church planter who gives a day a week to train others), but beyond that our structure is flat. As a relatively small group, everyone has a voice, but this is not to say that all voices are equal. Gifting, experience, and commitment to the movement identify certain members as authorities in certain areas, and so their voices may carry more weight.

Again, this is a dynamic wrought by the gospel. It is striking that early on in the expansion of the church, twice new churches were planted among new people groups by ordinary disciples and without the strategic input or authority of the apostles in Jerusalem: Philip preached the gospel and baptized believers in Samaria (Acts 8:4-13), and some unnamed disciples from Cyprus and Cyrene planted a church in Antioch (11:19-21). In both cases, it happened without the authorization or supervision of the Jerusalem apostles, who arrived only after the event. Their role was to observe what had taken place and affirm the progress in continuity with the work of the Spirit and the ministry of the risen Lord Jesus that began with them in Jerusalem (8:14; 11:22).

Whose decision was it to go to Samaria or Antioch? Who led the church-planting effort? Who authenticated the ministry? When Barnabas arrived from Jerusalem he "saw what the grace of God had done" (11:23).

Kingdom ownership. Though strong ownership of a shared vision is key in a healthy movement, a kingdom mindset that isn't concerned with boasting of achievements is also needed. A movement is not just self-sustaining but also self-effacing. It prizes invisibility and makes no claim to own the churches that belong or that are planted because of its existence. The movement exists for the kingdom of God, not to advance personal empires. It doesn't seek out partners to serve itself, but instead seeks to serve planters, churches, and networks through a quiet lattice of support, prayer, training, advice, resourcing, and so on.

The result is a movement that's other-church centered and made up of members happy to spend considerable time and energy establishing church plants beyond their own tribal boundaries. As Keller notes, "It leads to a culture of sacrificial commitment and intrinsic reward."[14] This invisibility is the mark of a movement eschewing status, brand development, and personal expansion, because the vision alone is compelling and its fulfillment reward enough.

If you were to ask how many churches 2020birmingham has planted, in a real sense the answer is none. No 2020birmingham church plant exists. What do exist are churches planted since 2010 that can testify to the role 2020birmingham has played in their formation, growth, and long-term health. We do run an annual conference to cast vision, and we celebrate what God has chosen to do, but we aren't well-known across the city or even among our church members. If we remain invisible, achieve our goals, kick-start a movement beyond us, and disappear without a trace, we trust we will be content.

Again, this invisibility is not just a healthy dynamic; it is a *gospel-wrought* dynamic. As Paul wrote, we are to do nothing out of selfish ambition or vain conceit. Rather, in humility we are to value others above ourselves, not looking to our own interests but each of us to the interests of others (Philippians 2:3-7). This is the example of Jesus, who made himself nothing, embracing obscurity, for the sake of lost men and women.

Flexibility. When the goal is the rapid multiplication of healthy, faithful churches across a city or region, flexibility is critical. Movements don't tell people how to plant churches, and diversity is celebrated. Why be flexible? Why take risks? Why "have a go"? As Paul wrote, the gospel demands it: "I have become all things to all people so that by all possible means I might save some. I do all this for the sake of the gospel, so that I may share in its blessing" (1 Corinthians 9:22-23).

Churches that are highly contextualized to their communities are well placed for mission. Their church plants are dynamic and innovative, and they often influence the whole church-planting movement. This requires both a strong commitment to mission and adaptive approaches to planting.[15] Then there is also flexibility when it comes to loyalty to the historic methodologies of the movement itself. The methods deployed to get to the point of planting a first new church may well need to change for further advancement. As the vision grows, the movement continually evolves and reinvents itself.

Within 2020birmingham this is evident in the sheer variety of church-planting models represented among us. All types of plant are encouraged and supported, whether they are pioneer, multisite, mother-daughter, replant, or revitalization. (For more information on these models, see table 3.1.) Each type of plant adopts a distinctive approach to church life and practice, from the more traditional—focused around a Sunday gathering—to expressions of the missional community model. We have assisted in non-English-speaking plants. We are always willing to try, to take risks, and to keep learning as we proceed.

Table 3.1. Models of church plants[16]

PLANT MODEL	EXPLANATION
Pioneer	Planting into new territory, typically without a direct sending church, made up of a core team gathered from a variety of places, around key leadership. Neil belongs to City Church, which began as a pioneer plant. It has since been involved in a variety of church-planting models.
Mother-Daughter	A church in one part of a town or city planting a new church sending a portion of its members, often with the goal of it becoming a fully autonomous congregation.
Multisite	A single church consisting of a number of congregations meeting in different locations, under a shared leadership.

On-Site Plant	A single church made up of multiple congregations, with distinct identities meeting at different times at the same site.
Replant	A church taking over the remnant of another church that has intentionally made the decision to close, in order to begin again in a new way.
Revitalization	A church intentionally embracing a process of significant change, usually beginning with new leadership, to recover a lost frontier for mission. John belongs to Crossway Church, which began as a church revitalization project.

Open membership, spontaneity and organic organization, leadership by influence, kingdom ownership, and flexibility—these dynamics may not be present in every movement that has ever existed, but in a healthy, vital church-planting movement, they assist in the fulfillment of the vision, and they flow out of the gospel itself. We aren't claiming to have mastered the research in this area, and we recognize that other criteria may come into play. We aren't attempting to be prescriptive or exhaustive, but neither are we being entirely anecdotal. These dynamics are being road-tested by 2020birmingham, while also being confirmed by other city movements around the world.[17]

Before we reach the end of this chapter, we want to advocate two distinctive features of the type of movement we're advocating: localism and collaboration. These two key ingredients mean a movement really does act together for the city.

Localism. Most networks and denominations tend to be national, or even international, in their scope. In fact, within many movements, becoming *global* is one of the clear objectives. And that is a truly noble goal. In this age of globalization, numerous church-planting networks have been astonishingly fruitful as they've planted churches across the world.

However, it's important to recognize that localism is a complementary and equally essential value. In fact, when we lose sight of the local, the overall cause is damaged. The benefits of a global reach aren't evenly distributed, so there are perils—and victims—of globalization.[18] A global vision needs local heroes. Otherwise, real communities and real people are left behind. And of course, globalism is the domain of Somewheres, not Anywheres, so those left behind are often the most vulnerable and disenfranchised members of society.

Just think of the benefits that could flow from a group of different churches meeting regularly to pray over the challenges and opportunities of reaching their particular community. A local movement creates an opportunity to rediscover this local focus and is energized by real relationships on the ground. Churches in a local movement can learn from one another, sharing ideas and resources along with local knowledge. Movements that prize generosity can become experts locally, giving away that knowledge base to others.

2020birmingham is aspiring to be a local movement. (The clue is in the name.) By being local, we feel our responsibility is to seek to do all that we can to reach our city for Christ. *All of it*—over a million people in distinct geographical, socioeconomic, and ethnic communities sprawling out over the Midlands of the United Kingdom.

Birmingham itself is made up of 167 distinct geographical neighborhoods. About twenty other larger regions make up the surrounding area, locally known as the Black Country because of the soot from the heavy industries established around coal mining in the nineteenth century. Beyond the English language, there are at least twenty other languages that over a thousand people living in the city speak as their primary mode of communication. Beyond them, over thirty thousand additional people speak still other languages.

Our seventeen church plants have only scratched the surface. Our vision for fifty churches that will plant churches feels like a good first stab, and we are palpably aware of our limitations. But we are committed to being local: slowing down, having our eyes opened to the beauty and the needs of our surroundings, and having our hearts toward our communities warmed.

[*Collaboration*] As gospel ministers laboring alongside one another, we often view each other as competition and with deep suspicion instead of seeing opportunity to collaborate. Movements can gather momentum quickly because they can partner across denominations and networks, working together for a single greater goal. The sum is very much greater than the parts. When a movement owns a compelling vision that's bigger than any single church or network could achieve, it *compels* transdenominational partnership. Quite simply, reaching a city with the gospel doesn't take just a movement; it takes a *collaborative* movement.

This way of thinking requires planters, networks, denominations, and parachurch organizations operating in the same context to be deliberate in seeking partnership. This vision compels everyone to look for opportunities to collaborate, to give time to building new relationships, to be driven by a conviction that so much more needs to be done than is being done and so much more can be done than could ever be done in isolation.

Collaboration is much more than the kind of fellowship we know well. There is a significant contrast between gatherings of churches for mutual encouragement and collaborating to create a local movement.[19] *Fellowship* gatherings share information and send leaders back inspired and refreshed. However, in *collaborative* movements, it isn't ideas alone that are shared. The collaborative outcome is joint ownership of a tangible greater *goal* that far exceeds the expectations of any individual church.

Collaboration always keeps the cause in sight. You are laboring together *to achieve something*. For example, Neil and I (John) may enjoy Christian fellowship, and we may also be partners in the gospel, but it required *collaboration* to write a book together. It required shared ownership of a single goal. In the context of a movement, that means churches agree to pray, work, and give to something bigger. It means when church leaders gather, there is less focus on the needs of the individuals and churches represented, and greater focus on the kingdom. In a network or a partnership, we each help the others to accomplish their goals, expecting them to do the same for us. In a collaborative movement, we work together to accomplish kingdom goals that we may not personally benefit from at all and that we could never achieve by ourselves.[20]

Daniel Yang, reflecting on his own experiences planting in Toronto within a multidenominational network, wrote, "A funny thing happens when you tell your church planters that they're allowed to learn and to play with other tribes and networks. Your church planters become more savvy in leadership and culture. And they end up having a bigger picture of what God is doing outside of their own church and their own denomination."[21]

We find this all the time. Spending time with people who think differently, pray differently, worship differently, ask different questions, identify different problems, seek different solutions, have different emphases, hold different opinions, and even notice different differences is, to be frank, exhilarating.

Collaboration is not just good fun; it is also a biblical principle. As the apostle Paul wrote,

What, after all, is Apollos? And what is Paul? Only servants, through whom you came to believe—as the Lord has assigned to each his task. I planted the seed, Apollos watered it, but God has been making it grow. So neither the one who plants nor the one who waters is anything, but only God, who makes things grow. The one who plants and the one who waters have one purpose, and they will each be rewarded according to their own labor. For we are co-workers in God's service; you are God's field, God's building. (1 Corinthians 3:5-9)

The church is described as a common field, and as gospel ministers we are the unskilled servants through whom God brings about growth. We are not anything—in fact, we are "the things that are not" (1:28)—*nothings* chosen by God so that we boast only in him. We are his servants, working in his field for his glory.

Because this is the way in which we are to understand gospel ministry, though we may have our own particular contribution to make, we share "one purpose" (3:8). We may be distinct ministers with distinct roles to be distinctly rewarded, but we are one, and we share a common vision.

By implication this means we shouldn't have an elevated view of our ministry. We must view ourselves together as "co-workers in God's service" (3:9). By this Paul didn't mean we're working alongside God but working alongside one another as those who belong to God. The principle of colaboring is at the heart of a right understanding of ministers and ministry. As David Garland reflected, "The field is not a battlefield where workers vie with one another for supremacy. It is a farmstead to be brought under cultivation so as to produce fruit (Matthew 21:43). If the farmhands do not work cooperatively, the crop will be ruined."[22]

None of this is to deny that the differences in our approaches to ministry are real and are arrived at by personal conviction. For example, as an individual we may be a convinced credobaptist or paedobaptist, continuationist or cessationist, because we believe it is what the Bible teaches. We may have actively ruled out joining particular denominations because we regard their polity as less than biblical.

Part two of this book will explain in detail how we approach collaboration in a way that seeks to respect the differences among us, but for now it's enough to say that our togetherness is an essential outworking of the gospel that's necessary to reach our city, and collaboration doesn't necessarily mean compromise.

Matthew 9:38 and Mark 9:38 (outlined in chapter one) should be ringing in our ears. The simple truth is that we are far too tribal, and tribalism is the consequence of failing to reflect deeply on the gospel. Tribalism is driven by self-preservation, but mission is driven by self-sacrifice. A tribal community exists solely for itself, but a missional community exists for others. A tribal mindset results in isolationism, but a missional mindset ought to produce the fruit of generous, self-effacing, risky, and surprising collaboration.

The author Matt Perman, writing about productivity, reflects, "God designed the world so that there will always be more things for us to do than we are able to do. This isn't just so we learn to prioritize; it's so that we learn to depend on one another."[23] Instead of thinking (to quote every Wild West movie), *This town ain't big enough for the both of us*, we should be thinking, *This field is far too big to farm without collaboration*. It has been said that there is no limit to what a person can do so long as they don't care a straw who gets the credit for it. If God would so choose to use them, local collaborative church-multiplication movements are uniquely placed to help his colaborers reach his field for his glory.

City Movements, Networks, and Denominations

By now it should be clear that defining a localized, collaborative church-planting movement as we have outlined above is not straightforward. It can be helpful to see how a city movement like 2020birmingham is different from networks like Acts 29, Ecclesia, Stadia, V3, and the Fellowship of Independent Evangelical Churches—plus denominational institutions such as the Southern Baptist North American Mission Board, the Church of England, and Anglican Mission in England. Table 3.2 highlights similarities and contrasts between the types of organizations. Inevitably this is an oversimplification, but we think it's a fair assessment of the differences.

Table 3.2. City movements, networks, and denominations

	CITY MOVEMENTS	NETWORKS	DENOMINATIONS
Membership	Open	Often Closed, but at times Open	Closed
Strategy	Spontaneous	Spontaneous	Planned
Organization	Organic	Simultaneously Organic and Structured	Structured
Leadership	Influence	May be Influence and/or Authority	Authority
Ownership	Kingdom	Often Kingdom, but at times Institution	Institution
Innovation	Flexible	Flexible	Traditional
Cooperation	Collaborative	Within own tribe	Within own tribe
Scope	Local/Regional	National/ International	National/ International

We've found it helpful to note that the categories in table 3.2 aren't mutually exclusive; there may well be crossover among them. For example, there may be times when a movement behaves like a network and times when a network may behave either like a movement or a denomination (see figure 3.1). At first sign, it can be difficult to see any real difference between a network with movement dynamics and a movement with network dynamics. But each approach makes distinctive contributions.

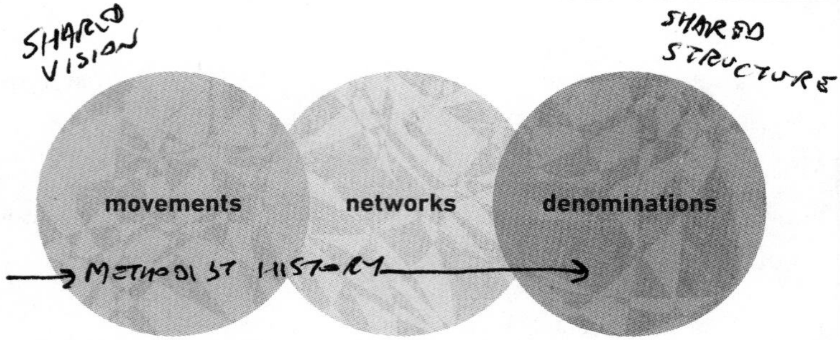
SHARED VISION
SHARED STRUCTURE
movements
networks
denominations
METHODIST HISTORY

Figure 3.1. Movements, networks, and denominations[24]

Our task is not to state in detail what networks and denominations are in their essence. It is to understand what a movement is. However, in table 3.2, it's evident that despite the crossover, each category has a particular collection of dynamics that helps to delineate what it is and where it provides a unique opportunity.

It can be particularly hard to see the distinction between movements and networks, but in terms of membership, ownership, cooperation, and scope, there should be some obvious differences in practice. In other areas, like strategy and innovation, networks may often exhibit the dynamics of movements, and at times movements may look remarkably like networks.

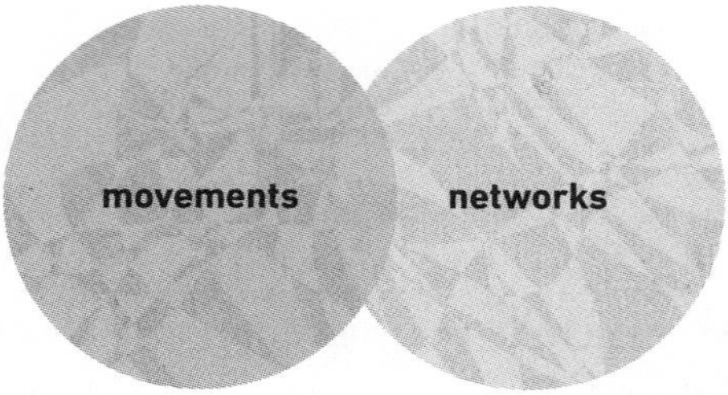
movements
networks

Figure 3.2. The overlap of movements and networks

It's also important to note that as movements begin to mature, they increasingly take on the characteristics of a network (see figure 3.3). The vitality and vision remain, but a greater degree of organization is required, appropriate leadership may begin to emerge, and structure may be added to serve the growth God gives.

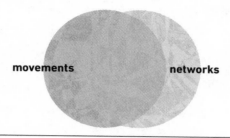

Figure 3.3. The overlap of mature movements and networks

One of the key things to note when comparing movements, networks, and denominations is that each sphere offers different strengths. Pay close attention here, as we don't want to be misunderstood at this point. Our claim is not that a church must choose which to belong to, but rather that a church plant may be nurtured, encouraged, and strengthened by belonging to more than one sphere. However, a church plant is especially and uniquely blessed by participation in a city movement, because this fosters a healthy localism that helps with strategy and contextualization and because it offers fruitful collaboration and peer-to-peer support with close neighbors.

Squares and Towers

In his fascinating book *The Square and the Tower*, Niall Ferguson uses the Italian city of Siena as an analogy for the differences between networks and hierarchies. For the sake of clarity, Ferguson uses *network* as a broad term with many varieties, which would include what we are calling *networks* and *movements* in this book. He describes the Piazza del Campo, a large public square in the shadow of the Torre del Mangia, a tall tower built by the civic authorities of Siena, and notes, "Nowhere in the world will you see so elegantly juxtaposed the two forms of human organization . . . around you, a public space purpose-built for all kinds of more or less informal human interaction; above you, an imposing tower intended to symbolize and project secular power."[25] Coincidentally, the clock tower in the center of the University of Birmingham in our own city is modeled after Siena's Torre del Mangia, and the university campus reflects a near-identical dynamic.

It would be wrong to pit the square against the tower. Ferguson gives a breathtaking tour of the tension between the two throughout world history before effectively concluding, "The world remains a world of squares *and* towers."[26] 2020birmingham is a public square where any number of networks, denominations, hierarchies, and movements can interact at the local church level. Ferguson carefully explains that it matters how dense a network is and how connected it is to other clusters. He observes that the ability to "go viral" is most likely where both strong and weak ties within and across networks allow for horizontal peer-to-peer links.[27] If this is true, then the kind of movement described in this chapter may be just the environment to birth a healthy epidemic of church planting—or better, an explosion of joy that could reach a whole city for Jesus.

Conclusion

We hope that what we've outlined above won't be dismissed as a fad. Movements aren't this year's Harlem Shake, a fad that's far outdated as we write. We've argued that the essence of any true movement is an internal vitality spurred by a compelling vision. Alongside this, healthy spiritual movements also foster a dynamic of open membership, spontaneity and organic organization, leadership by influence, kingdom ownership, and flexibility. And in order to reach a community comprehensively, they will also emphasize localism and collaboration.

These should not be thought of as merely alternative ways for churches to work together, driven only by pragmatic considerations. True spiritual movements exhibit the same dynamics evident in the birth and global expansion of the church. They find their earliest expression in the Spirit-led explosive growth of the church in the book of Acts. There should be an organic, self-propagating, dynamic power always at work within the church. In Acts, the good news spread essentially on its own, with little institutional support or embodiment, and without strategic plans or the control of managers.[28] Local collaborative church multiplication movements are, therefore, a desire to see God work in our day and age in ways testified to in the birth of the church.

In saying all of this, we aren't seeking to dismiss in any way the role networks and denominations play. There is no need to choose between them. There may be important reasons to find a home within the "tower" of a denominational structure, while also harnessing the benefits and blessings of the "square" of a movement. Movements do not make networks and denominations redundant; they complement them and offer a unique and necessary opportunity for the evangelization of our nations, one community at a time.

PART 2

How

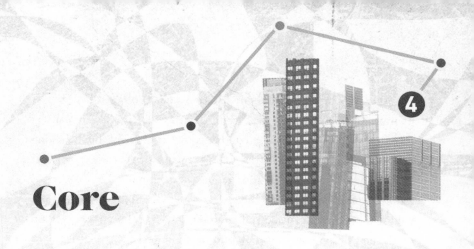

Core

This chapter will cover the following:

- *the first term of the equation for collaboration, which is a shared core of beliefs rooted in the gospel;*
- *how there are two ways to get the gospel wrong, and how we guard against each;*
- *how there's the difference between the goal of ecumenism and the goal of collaboration around core beliefs; and*
- *how this shared core of beliefs rooted in the gospel serves as a movement boundary.*

I (John) was talking recently with two church leaders from very different networks, both ministering in the same northern city in England.

Together they had just cast their vision for a local collaborative church-planting movement. They were visiting our 2020birmingham planters' forum out of curiosity, having together committed themselves to seeing thirty churches planted in the neediest parts of their city by 2030. They'd also sent out an invitation to a conversation to a large variety of local church leaders and had three clear responses: Some churches were willing to lend them an ear, and around thirty-five churches turned up on the day. Other churches took offense at the presence of a statement of faith and their apparent theological narrowness. Other churches made it clear they wouldn't be sending anyone to consider something so broad and inclusive.

It may be tempting to view this as a failure at the first hurdle. But perhaps it's a sign they pitched it right. It certainly revealed that collaboration has its challenges.

Most people are convinced in theory that collaboration is a worthy aim. In part one we briefly recalled the events of Dunkirk. The "Dunkirk spirit" has been defined as a "willingness by a group of people in a bad situation to all help each other."[1] Dunkirk is a breathtaking example of what's possible when people are willing to serve a bigger vision beyond themselves, but it isn't just national emergencies that draw people together. In fact, collaboration has never been more talked about and utilized than right now. TED Talks has more than 180 videos on the subject. Whether it be cross-party alliances within politics, a strategy to combat the next deadly virus, open-sourcing to generate better ideas, the birth of Wikipedia, or the sharing economy of Uber and Airbnb, collaboration is the trend du jour.

Collaboration has been identified as the secret to responding to a need quickly and competently. For example, Stanford Business recently reported on the Nature Conservancy, an environmental group seeking to cultivate change through a collaborative movement, saying,

"We can scale our ability to tackle the causes we care about, faster and more effectively by collaborating rather than scaling from within."[2] Collaboration also unlocks avenues for development and growth. *Harvard Business Review* cited the example of the healthcare industry, where technology, consumer electronics, and a medical device company have collaborated to improve patient care postsurgery: "No one or two of these companies could have brought this idea to market without the assets and unique expertise of the others."[3]

The world is learning to collaborate, but what about the church? Surely the need is greater for the church and the cause even more compelling. So why did two church leaders in a northern city in England face pushback the moment they cast the vision? There is both a negative and a positive answer.

Negatively, we're often unwilling to look beyond our differences in order to collaborate. We don't allow the gospel to go deeply enough for us to see the need and opportunity in front of us. The example of the world rightly shames us into considering whether there is more that we could do together.

Positively, we're right to be careful about who we collaborate with. We aren't mere pragmatists, willing to do anything to serve a cause we believe in. The principle of fidelity is primary.

What was it that got Jonathan Bell and I (Neil) to have that first coffee together? We were an unlikely pair. We had never met, had no natural context to create a partnership, and had planted very different churches. As busy pastors, neither of us was looking for additional people to drink coffee with.

In the first instance, we respected each other enough to take the time to discover what we had in common. And what we had in common was greater than what separated us, as important as those things were to us as individuals. What we quickly realized was that we shared the same vision because we shared the same gospel, and it had gone deeply in the same way. Our vision for the city wasn't driven by a desire to make much of ourselves but to make much of Jesus. This overcame the positive barrier to collaboration: we knew that whatever the things were that separated us, we had a shared core of beliefs rooted in the gospel.

It would have been easy for Jonathan and me to have judged one another by a different set of criteria. For me, it would have been a fear of Jonathan seeking to turn me into an arm-waving, tongue-speaking charismatic; for Jonathan, it would have been my theological conservatism and love of checked shirts.

More seriously, it's often not so much the individuals themselves that cause suspicion but the people with whom we associate or the groups to which we belong. Despite our differences, Jonathan and I both belong to evangelical networks. It would have been tempting for us to be wary of seeking collaboration with an evangelical who belonged to a mixed denomination. This so-called "second-degree separation" could sap the life from any attempt at generous active partnership.

Jonathan wrote about the barriers he himself had to overcome:

While it might be relatively easy to *inspire* you with stories of what we're doing, *convince* you theologically that it's really important, and provide all the practical *advice* you need to get started—in my experience, the biggest obstacle to actually doing anything about all of this has been the state of my own heart! In short, I want to look good, and I want the church I lead to flourish because it reflects well on me. Or, to dress it up in slightly more acceptable vocabulary, the church I lead has a big vision, and I'm at full capacity serving the church! Either way, because of my insecurities, I need the church to succeed so that I look like I'm being successful.

Which means that if it's a choice between giving my time to my church or the church down the road, I'm always going to prioritize my own church. Or if the church is already stretched in terms of people and finance, I'm hardly going to encourage anyone to move to join a church plant on the other side of the city. Or if a new church plant starts right on our doorstep, I'm going to feel threatened and unhappy!

And so I might say I'm really supportive of city movements (and I might really like the idea in *theory*); but in *practice*, I don't want anyone else to prosper at the expense of the church I lead.

However, what I've come to see is the gospel sets me free from this need to overcome, triumph, and perform better than everyone else. I don't have to compete against others for my worth, because God has already proven it through the cross. I have absolutely nothing to prove and so I'm now set free to pour myself out for others. What's more, at the end of time, Jesus is returning for a glorious bride made up of every church. I don't know about you, but I want to devote myself to the building up, flourishing, and health of the whole—not just my little bit!

Though there are many examples of collaboration in the world, when you probe a bit, the vast majority aren't truly altruistic. Collaboration often exists because it's in the personal interest of both parties. At times it hides a disharmony and clash of values under the surface, and the collaboration may be short-lived before a competitive stance returns. The example of the world rightly warns us that pure utilitarianism can't be the goal. Both *means* and *ends* matter.

When we evoke the Dunkirk spirit and speak of responding to the urgent need with "anything that will float," there's a danger that will be heard as "anything that works." However, the goal is not simply a tally of church plants; it's healthy churches for the long term. Vessels that are letting in water aren't fit for their purpose. As we saw in chapter one, the principle of urgency flows from fidelity to Christ; it should not be used to undermine it.

All of this brings us to the first term of our collaboration equation: *core*. For churches to embark on collaboration, there must first be a common core: a simple, clear, shared articulation of the gospel.

Two Ways to Get the Gospel Wrong

There is only one gospel, and it is true, unchanging, and free. Paul's letter to the Galatian church is a magnificent treatise written to defend the truth that "a person is not justified by works of the law, but by faith in Jesus Christ" (Galatians 2:16). As wonderful as the truth is, have you ever noticed that in that letter Paul highlighted how it's possible to deny the gospel in two different ways because of an unhealthy approach to collaboration. We can be *too broad* and partner with those who don't believe the gospel, and we can be *too narrow* and refuse to partner with those who do believe the gospel.

Throughout this little letter, Paul celebrated this gospel of freedom, in which we are justified by faith alone in Christ alone. We are made right with God through faith in the Son of God, who loved us and gave himself for us. We are children of God through faith, clothed with him, so that we are all one in Christ Jesus. And so, we're never to boast in anything except the cross of our Lord Jesus Christ.

Paul explained that "false believers had infiltrated our ranks to spy on the freedom we have in Christ Jesus and to make us slaves" (Galatians 2:4). The result of this is Paul's record of his diplomatic mission to Jerusalem. His trip was not to seek validation for his message from the other apostles but to ensure that the church would stand by him as a true apostle, by his message as the true gospel, and by new believers, Jew and Gentile alike, as the true people of God.

At stake was nothing less than "the truth of the gospel" (2:5), and the freedom that accompanies it.

Paul celebrated this gospel, but he also guarded its truth like a Rottweiler. He was perplexed that the Gentiles in Galatia were in danger of throwing away their freedom. He wrote, "I am astonished that you are so quickly deserting the one who called you to live in the grace of Christ and are turning to a different gospel—which is really no gospel at all" (1:6-7). He warned against setting aside the grace of God (2:21). And he challenged them, "Now that you know God—or rather are known by God—how it is that you are turning back to those weak and miserable forces?" (4:9). Paul put it starkly: to deny the gospel and to seek to be justified by one's own effort is to be alienated from Christ and to have fallen away from grace (5:4).

How were the Galatians doing this? By being tempted to welcome, partner with, and affirm false teachers. The major thrust of the letter to the Galatians was to make them as a church very aware of the danger of compromising the gospel through collaboration that's broader than the gospel allows. The "circumcision group" are gospel deniers, and the church can't partner with them. It would be utterly inappropriate for Paul to have encouraged some kind of unity with them.

Elsewhere, in relation to false teachers, Paul wrote, "Have nothing to do with such people" (2 Timothy 3:5). Don't collaborate! In fact he described them as agitators he wished "would go the whole way and emasculate themselves!" (Galatians 5:12). This is not simply a crude jibe but a genuine desire that the ministry of those distorters of the gospel would not succeed but would shrivel up and perish, and no longer produce children of Hagar: children of slavery (see 4:21-31).

Paul was a freedom fighter. He didn't seek to find common ground with false teachers—or encourage the church to either. No, he said, "We did not give in to them for a moment, so that the truth of the gospel might be preserved for you" (2:5). If we can't agree on the gospel, we can't be united. To partner with gospel deniers is to get the gospel wrong.

There have certainly been conversations in 2020birmingham about whether or not a shared core of beliefs rooted in the gospel among planters is present or not. In one particular instance, a planter shared a desire to reach the city and to some extent shared the DNA of the movement more generally, but amid their core beliefs was a position on human sexuality that contradicted clear biblical teaching and was fundamentally a disagreement on the gospel.

When it comes to collaboration, the question of how broad we can be without undermining the gospel requires careful reflection and an answer that sits well with the conscience of all involved. For 2020birmingham, this has meant we are evangelical and not Roman Catholic or liberal in theology.[4] We are traditional and not "open and affirming" on matters of human sexuality. When it comes to the role of men and women in ministry we recognize that people within 2020birmingham may themselves be egalitarian and belong to networks that would train women as lead planters. Yet, we would not seek to raise up and train women as lead planters within 2020birmingham because many within the movement are complementarian. This leads to a further question. *Who decides* how broad we can be? In a context where movement dynamics are being nurtured, there's a desire to keep hierarchy as flat as possible. So the organization is a square, not a tower. However, a free-for-all, being open to all comers without any rules, would only result in confusion and ambiguity. For us, it made sense for those closest the center—the catalysts of the movement—to be the ones to define the core—and therefore the boundary.

We can lose the gospel by being too broad, but we can also lose the gospel by refusing to partner with those who do believe the gospel.

And it's the nature of Paul's confrontation with his fellow apostle Peter that makes this point clear. When Peter came to the church in Antioch, rather than eating with Gentile believers as he always had, he began to separate himself from them out of fear of the circumcision group. Paul said Peter "stood condemned" (Galatians 2:11). Why? Because he denied the gospel not in word but in action. The Judaizers were mistaken at the level of their theology, but Peter's theology was most certainly orthodox; yet he had got the gospel wrong in practice. The truth of the gospel he affirmed with his lips simply had not gone deep enough. It was his "hypocrisy" (2:13), not heresy, that was at the heart of the issue. Peter believed the gospel but was not "acting in line with the truth of the gospel" (2:14).

What Peter demonstrated is the contradiction that can lie buried in the heart of an evangelical orthodoxy. Perhaps our greatest danger then is that it is quite possible to get the gospel wrong even as we hold on to justification by faith through Christ alone. We get it wrong when we live in a manner that contradicts or denies it. Paul opposed Peter in Antioch because, although he still believed in justification by faith, he was no longer willing to eat with Gentile believers. Peter had decided to separate himself from these Christians because they were not circumcised. Unity, in practice, had become conditional on *more* than fidelity; other boxes needed to be ticked. For Peter to refuse to partner with gospel affirmers was as wrong-headed and damaging to the gospel as the Galatian temptation to partner with gospel deniers.

Within conservative schools of evangelicalism, we're rightly concerned about partnerships between those who clearly do not profess the same faith. We're concerned that the gospel should not be too broad. But do we share the same concern about denying the gospel with our actions? Do we refuse to consider partnership with other believers simply because we don't share the same view of every secondary issue?

We more easily see that we can be *too broad* and partner with those who don't believe the gospel. This, we know, compromises the gospel. However, we find it harder to see that we can also be *too narrow* when we refuse to partner with those who do believe the gospel. And this, too, compromises the truth we profess.

So, on the one side, some of us may be tempted to partner without any true unity in the one Lord Jesus Christ. We may be tempted to seek unity at the expense of truth and in doing so fall away from grace. We may want the illusion of a Dunkirk spirit, when we actually belong to different sides. Others of us need to see the equal and opposite challenge to not make the gospel too narrow. Like Paul we are freedom fighters, ready to take on anyone or anything that may undermine the gospel of grace, but we aren't ready to give an expression to the unity we have with fellow believers. Instead we want to play it safe by narrowing our allegiances, and we end up fencing a large number of brothers and sisters from the table simply because they don't think, speak, and act like we do. We refuse to launch with the other vessels because we don't like the color of their sails, their style of piloting, or the cut of their jib.

When we get the gospel right—when we are neither too broad nor too narrow—it results in a fidelity that says it's only with those in Christ that we can experience true unity. It also results in a humility that says we have no better standing before God than anyone else. In the end, this results in a generosity that says everyone in Christ is welcome. It results in a unity where we put aside our secondary differences and celebrate the truth of the gospel and the freedom to be one people in the Lord Jesus Christ.

A while ago Abraham, one of our church planters, raised an issue during the 2020birmingham planters forum. The Ethiopian Evangelical Church he had helped to plant was growing fast, and they desperately needed to find a larger and more suitable meeting space. We set to work praying, and a solution began to emerge. The Anglican bishop of Aston (in Birmingham) had previously spoken at one of our conferences as someone with church-planting experience within the Church of England denomination. He knew 2020birmingham and was excited by the vision and the green shoots that were emerging.

On his own, Abraham would have struggled to know who to approach or how to approach them, but Neil was able to write to the bishop and inquire on his behalf. The bishop demonstrated generosity and willingness to help—without any reluctance at all—and was able to broker a deal that allowed the church to meet in a Church of England building where it could continue to grow. Three different parties got the gospel right.

While we have our own convictions about ecclesiology, spiritual gifts, predestination, the days of creation, and modes of baptism, getting the gospel right means also being ready to accept anyone and everyone who is in Christ as our brother and sister. We will relate to others in a way that suggests we really believe that God has no favorites, regardless of race, gender, language, or color of skin, and regardless of whether or not someone speaks in tongues or has ever heard of the Christian books we have read.

When the core is clear, faithful local churches won't be in competition with each other. American theologian Albert Barnes reflected on these truths from Galatians and stated, "Let there be a disposition to rejoice in the talents, and zeal, and success of others, though it should far outstrip our own,—and contention in the church would cease; and every devoted and successful minister of the gospel would receive the right hand of fellowship from all . . . who love the cause of true religion."[5]

What we are together in Christ is so much more important than all the things we use to separate us. The gospel compels our unity, and our mission demands it. As Ryken wrote, "The evangelization of the world depends on this kind of cooperation in the church. Rather than taking pride in our own ministry, we should celebrate what God is doing through others. . . . We not only allow for . . . differences, but rejoice in them, provided that we are all preaching the same gospel."[6] With a clear core, the cause is not a context for contest but for Christ-honoring collaboration.

This is what Jonathan and I (Neil) have discovered. We aren't naive; we understand that the differences we have are real—and important. But we accept each other as brothers in Christ. A good example of the trust we have, despite our theological particularities, is that though we wouldn't make the other's church our spiritual home, we've been invited to preach in the other's context. We've worked hard to make the core clear, and we have confidence in each other's ministries. This is the first step toward healthy collaboration.

No Undercover Ecumenism

It's important to state at this point that we aren't advocating some kind of under-the-radar ecumenical movement. Modern ecumenism has the expressed goal of deepening the communion of all churches leading to a common witness and service.[7] It pursues this goal by deliberately *not* articulating a basis of faith beyond a simple "statement of intent." This allows churches to display a kind of public unity together without necessarily agreeing on a common core. There are a number of difficulties with this.

First, in terms of its articulation of the gospel, it necessarily becomes too reductionistic. It would happily include any church that calls itself Christian, without any shared grasp of the heart of the gospel. However, what Jonathan and I (Neil) are seeking to demonstrate is that for a true Christ-centered movement to begin, it must be both gospel-centered and gospel-driven, so that grace defines and empowers all we seek to do.

Second, the ecumenical movement's goal is common witness and service. It is striving for an organic unity that would eventually eradicate the distinctives of its constituent members. For ecumenism to flourish, denominational groupings and networks are considered to be divisions that must be overcome and eventually removed. On the contrary, within a movement, unity doesn't equal uniformity. An appropriate degree of unity can be sought while respecting the diversity of theological opinion among its partners. The goal isn't to eradicate distinctives but to celebrate them, because a strength comes when people think and act very differently from one another while working together. It's striking that in Ephesians 4 Paul appeared to make a distinction between the "unity of the Spirit" that we have by virtue of our salvation and that we must make every effort to keep (Ephesians 4:3), and the "unity of the faith," which is something we are growing in as we strive toward "the whole measure of the fullness of Christ" (4:13).

Third, the ecumenical endeavor is the proclamation of the gospel by common witness. The belief is that Christian mission is enhanced as we rise above the distinctives and limitations of the local church. However, within a movement, the mission of the local church is paramount. Churches do not exist to serve the movement; the movement exists to serve the churches. Within 2020birmingham we understand that we aren't planting churches together, but together are planting churches. This may sound pedantic, but it's a key way we retain an appropriately modest unity, celebrate denominational and network distinctives, and retain the strength and autonomy of the local church—all the while harnessing the blessings of real collaboration.

The Core of Collaboration

In figure 4.1, which will be discussed and developed over the next couple of chapters, we see that the core of collaboration functions counterintuitively as a boundary for the movement. Churches marked A, B, and C share the common core; they are faithful to the gospel. Churches marked D and E do not share the common core of gospel convictions.

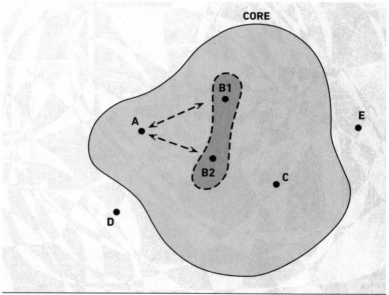

Figure 4.1. The core of collaboration

At this point, the churches inside the boundary do not belong to any kind of movement, but they are all churches that could at least potentially find ways of collaborating. Churches B1 and B2 belong to the same denomination, and they enjoy informal fellowship with A from time to time. Church C is affiliated with a network that tends to function on its own, and there isn't much of a relationship in place yet.

Figure 4.1 attempts to display what many of us already experience day to day in our local context. We have connections with a number of other churches on the ground, and we have it because of our common core. These are the ones we're in the circle with. We may at times meet together, perhaps for prayer, encouragement, and training. This kind of fellowship is an extremely positive end in itself, and our intention is not to undermine that or see it as anything other than a great blessing.

However, the "core" alone may generate fellowship but not collaborative action—and movements are all about action. As blessed as fellowship is, it can also be dangerous. Perhaps you've been in contexts where fellowship has turned sour through comparison games and one-upmanship. That can be an attempt to feel strong and to mask weakness. Conversation may fall into self-congratulation rather than cultivating a brokenheartedness for our city. At these times, our fellowship can distract us from the spiritual need and opportunity before us.

Core is the first and essential term of the equation, and it provides the foundation for a collaborative movement. Fellowship grows into more with the presence of the second term of our equation: *cause* (the subject of the next chapter), which provides the focus.[8]

Identifying a core of beliefs rooted in the gospel and common to two very different churches comes first—and it's dynamite. As Paul wrote, "So in Christ Jesus you are all children of God through faith, for all of you who were baptized into Christ have clothed yourselves with Christ" (Galatians 3:26-27). In a city where there are about ninety reported incidents of a hate crime each week, let me (John) share with you a tiny glimpse of what it means for us to be "one in Christ Jesus" (3:28). I have the privilege of leading a church that owns a rather dilapidated building, but one that has its own baptism pool. A number of church plants have used the building on Sunday afternoons to hold baptism services, because they lack the facilities themselves.

One of those baptisms will stay with me forever. The Ethiopian Evangelical Church of Birmingham booked the building for a couple of hours one Sunday afternoon. I arrived to open up at the agreed-on hour, but my watch was set to English time instead of African. The service got going roughly around the time we had agreed to close up again. So, after an English display of frustration ("It's absolutely no trouble at all"), I relaxed, loitered at the back, and began to take it in. I lost count of how many baptisms took place that afternoon, but what I witnessed was the most exuberant display of joy in the Lord Jesus a white man from Yorkshire had ever seen. As those young Ethiopian and Eritrean men and women sang together, were baptized, and were prayed for—all in their mother tongue—I could see that as different as we were, we wore the same Christ clothes.

Cause

Attempt great things for God,
expect great things from God.

WILLIAM CAREY

This chapter covers these points:

- *how the second term of the equation for collaboration is a shared cause;*
- *how a shared theological vision produces the cause for a movement;*
- *how partnering at the level of doctrinal distinctives (level one), the level of ministry expression (level two), and the level of theological vision (level three) are different; and*
- *how level-three partnerships' contributions to localized movements are different.*

Imagine the following scenario, which is based on a number of true stories in Birmingham. A young church planter from another nation arrives in the city. He has no relationship with any local churches but knows that God has called him to establish a ministry among a particular community that UK planters are struggling to reach. He arrives out of necessity, as an asylum seeker, and discovers that his displacement was a divine appointment in the hands of a sovereign God. He is a missionary at heart, so he arrives envisioned and seeking to share the gospel. Having identified that his mother tongue has equipped him to be the best instrument to reach a whole community, he lives in that part of the city.

As he begins, he meets a number of barriers. He finds that as a single planter, he is very quickly at capacity and has no support structure around him to help with the load. He finds it difficult to rent somewhere to meet, get the word out about what his fledgling church is doing, and raise support for the growing work. He's easily misunderstood by other local churches and viewed with suspicion, because the church he's establishing is culturally very different from those in the United Kingdom.

He quickly feels unsupported and isolated. It isn't necessarily that he's unconnected to a denomination. It's just that, with all the vision in the world, it's hard to go it alone in another culture, thousands of miles from home.

At this point, he makes contact with a local church that belongs to 2020birmingham. Slowly a local collaboration emerges. That local church first becomes a supportive partner, simply praying for the work and offering practical help where possible. Then the planter becomes part of the church's leadership team, where he can be accountable and receive resources while he continues his work. The planter and the church begin to think about how they may find a way to establish the ministry together for the long term. The planter immediately has access to peer-to-peer support and to a wide network for prayer

support, mentoring, accountability, resources, and training. He joins
Incubator (the planters training program) and the planters forum.

Perhaps most importantly, he discovers there's a group of friends in the
city who don't view him and his work with suspicion. Instead they are
delighted God has sent him. The local church has the confidence to offer
help and to embark on the collaboration because they belong to a fledgling
movement of churches with a shared body of knowledge, and they and
the planter know there's somewhere to turn if things get difficult.

It sounds idyllic, but of course the reality is messy. Picture the logis-
tical complications of two congregations trying to work out how they
may share a building. Picture the interaction of two very different communities as they work out how to sing together, pray together, and grow
together. Picture an elders meeting where patience is wearing thin, as-
sumptions are being made about one another, and the cost of collaborating is being felt with some regret. Picture the finance meeting where
budgets are being projected, faith is waning, and brows are increasingly
furrowed. Picture a planter and a local church, both beginning to wonder
if it would've been a lot easier if they'd just continued to go it alone.

Why do they remain convinced that collaboration is worth the
effort? Where others may respectfully keep their distance, wish each
other well, and pursue their own interests, why do these two entities
continue to believe they are better together? It's too simplistic to conclude that they have a shared core of gospel-wrought convictions.
There's a second ingredient at work: a shared cause. Yes, they have a
shared vision of Christ, but they also have a shared vision for the city.

Cause

Paul began Colossians with these words: "To God's holy people in
Colossae, the faithful brothers and sisters in Christ" (Colossians 1:2).
He put two addresses on the letter he sent. Each believer and each

local church inhabits two locations: they are in Christ, and they are in a geographical community—in this case, Colossae.

The previous chapter identified the *core* that places us in Christ. This chapter is about the other address: our geographical location. If the previous chapter was the answer to the question "What does it mean to be in Christ?" this chapter answers the question "What does it mean to be in Christ *at this time and in this place?*"

I (John) first arrived in the city of Birmingham in 1997. I was eighteen, had been a Christian for about six months, and had never experienced city life before. I was used to the rural, coastal village life in Yorkshire, and moving into a predominantly Asian Muslim and urban community on the east side of this sprawling metropolis blew my mind. A year later I was living near the University of Birmingham, studying and then working for a church. Then I married, got a job, had a family, and so on. But in one unified sense my Christian walk has been all about answering the question above: What does it mean for me to be in *Christ* in the *twenty-first century* in the city of *Birmingham?*

I (Neil) grew up in Birmingham, not a Christian, and came to faith as a student in London while studying for a business degree. I returned to my city with my eyes opened; I just saw things differently. I had grown up in a blue-collar, working-class community without any kind of Christian witness, and it wasn't difficult to think of people in many other parts of the city facing the same situation. What would it mean for me to be in *Christ* in the *twenty-first century* in the city of *Birmingham?*

The same question applies more broadly. Every faithful church shares the same essential core but must grapple with the implications of the gospel as a community *at this time and in this place*. This is the *cause*. For 2020birmingham, it's nothing short of seeing the entire city of Birmingham reached with the gospel in our time. This is what we pray we're moving toward. With the bigger, box-C vision of chapter one in place, *cause* becomes a compelling term in the equation contributing to collaboration.

Level-Three Partnerships

A significant discovery for 2020birmingham was that partnerships between churches can happen on three different levels. The first two levels are common, logical, and form quite easily. However, there's a potential third level of partnership that's harder to realize; but once established, it can be incredibly fruitful. It's harder because it's concerned with an invisible step that we'll explain below. It's fruitful because it allows for collaboration between churches that don't see themselves as natural partners.

Table 5.1. Partnership levels and their contribution to church planting

PARTNERSHIP	EXAMPLE	DISTINCTIVE CONTRIBUTION TO CHURCH PLANTING
Level One	Denominational or network affiliation—e.g., FIEC, Church of England, New Frontiers	Assessment and convictions with regard to what you believe and why. Resources both in terms of money and recruitment
Level Two	Ministry expression and broader partnership—e.g., Together for the Gospel, Gospel Coalition	A clear philosophy of ministry, training, peer-to-peer support, worked examples
Level Three	Movement around a theological vision—e.g., 2020birmingham, City to City	A contextualized and coherent strategy for a specific time and place in order to reach a city or region for Christ

Level-one partnerships. Level-one partnerships describe churches in the same denomination or affiliation. They unite churches who celebrate identical—or at least very close—doctrinal beliefs and convictions.

Though churches in the same denomination share theological convictions, they can look very different when it comes to ministry practice. How is such a difference accounted for? Our ministry practices are never simply the result of our core theological convictions. Our theological vision is also at work. More on that will be said later in this chapter. One could—and should—expect two churches signed up to the same statement of faith but existing in two different cultural settings to arrive at different ministry outcomes.

Level-two partnerships. These partnerships are broader and encompass churches outside a single tradition. They tend to focus on a combination of shared theological convictions and ministry expressions. For example, churches with a commitment to Scripture that's expressed in a high view of expository preaching may choose to come together for training in Word-based ministry. A good example of such a partnership in the United Kingdom is the regional Gospel Partnerships, which bring together churches with similar convictions on Bible-handling. Made up largely of Reformed Anglican and Free churches, their differences prevent them coming together to celebrate all denominational distinctives. Their views on baptism or ecclesiology are diverse, but they can come together to train around shared ministry practices. In the United States, Together for the Gospel (T4G) is an example of a level-two partnership. Pastors across denominational traditions partner to host a conference that reaffirms and reiterates the central doctrines of the Christian faith.[1] The Gospel Coalition also comes under this category as a fellowship of evangelical churches in the Reformed tradition that exists to serve and resource churches regardless of denominational affiliation.[2]

Level-three partnerships. These partnerships are broader still than levels one or two. They do not choose to focus on doctrinal distinctives or particular ministry expressions but on questions of *theological vision.* A shared commitment to core evangelical convictions is essential, as we've already noted, but what compels the partnership is a desire to work through and work out all the complexities of being a faithful and effective gospel church in a particular time and place. So church planters seeking to work in the same city may come from a variety of different tribes (Presbyterian, Pentecostal, Baptist, Anglican, etc.), and because they share a very similar theological vision—the same values, emphases, and philosophy of ministry—it draws them into a fruitful partnership.

In the case of a church-planting cooperative, the theological vision brings into focus a very specific goal of planting across a region or a city. It isn't a level-one partnership, because there may be doctrinal distinctives that come to the fore in other contexts that are not pursued here. It isn't a level-two partnership, because unity doesn't require uniformity. These churches and planters will be working to establish churches quite different from one another in ethos and style. The shape of the plant itself varies significantly from church to church. It's a level-three partnership because, despite these differences, there's a deep conviction that more can be done together to serve a common cause than any level-one or level-two partnership could achieve on its own. Level-three partnerships in no way undermine the priority of theological commitment, but they allow churches to collaborate with a clear goal across the breadth of evangelicalism.

Partnership at level three is the key distinguishing feature of a movement over and against a network, a denomination, a gospel partnership, or a fellowship. Those take place at level one or two. A level-three partnership doesn't undermine other partnerships but allows a space for the movement dynamics (explored in chapter two) to be cultivated in terms of membership, strategy, organization, leadership, ownership, and innovation.

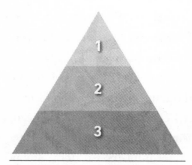
Figure 5.1. Pyramid of partnership

It might be helpful to see this as a pyramid of partnership. See figure 5.1. It's important to avoid viewing these three levels of partnership as a hierarchy. And the shape of the diagram is not designed to represent importance or even priority. A partnership around doctrinal convictions is not better or worse than one around a theological vision. But the pyramid does help us recognize two realities.

First, there is a natural order in which partnership is typically pursued. We, for the most part, identify in the first instance with a denomination or affiliation. We then may go on to develop relationships with other like-minded evangelicals. These form around ministry expressions that interest or concern us (preaching, worship, leadership structures, forms of mission and outreach). So we work at level 1 and level 2, but for many it stops there. In this book, we are making the case for actively pursuing level-3 partnerships, in particular, collaborative church-planting movements. Our experience suggests that in most of our minds it is a much bigger decision to work at level 3 than at levels 1 and 2.

Secondly, the triangle represents the breadth of partnership. In any given city, level 1 invites us to work with a small number of very like-minded churches. Level 2 opens the door to a greater number, and level 3 invites a partnership with a significant number of quite different churches.

We enjoy working in each of these three different partnerships as they accomplish different ends. In the context of church planting, partnerships at each level all have an important contribution to make.

Adding Cause to Core

The order of these first two terms of the collaboration equation is important. In their book on gospel partnerships, Bruno and Dirks distinguish between *foundation* and *focus.* They explain that kingdom partnerships usually focus on one specific implication of the gospel—for example, assisting the poor locally or overseas, influencing one area of culture, or teaching biblical interpretation to emerging church leaders. However, they warn that these implications of the gospel may be the *focus* of a partnership but they can't be the *foundation*. Put another way, a common *cause* can't be used to mask the lack of a clear common *core*.

We saw in the previous chapter that a common core that doesn't lead to a common cause can carry dangers as it becomes insular, masking weaknesses and failing to see the need of the city. But the opposite is even worse; a shared cause without a shared core is terminal. If implications of the gospel are all that holds us together, rather than the gospel itself, the ministry will fall apart as soon as the money runs out or differences relating to praxis arise, as they always do. For any movement to be self-sustaining in the long run, it can't afford to assume the gospel. There should be a direct line between the cause of the partnership and the explicit heart of the gospel: Jesus' life, death, and resurrection.[3] As Bruno and Dirks put it, "The gospel unites leaders and churches in a way that no philosophy, tradition, task, or mission ever could."[4]

We could say the gospel is even more crucial than that because the cause is itself empowered by the gospel. The true cause of a spiritual movement will be both centered around the gospel and driven by the gospel. To be gospel-centered is to have the gospel as the *core*, as described in chapter four. The gospel defines who we are and what we exist for. To be gospel-driven is to have the gospel empower the *cause*, as outlined in this chapter and the next. For this reason, the whole journey begins with fidelity to Christ.

The book of Acts makes this point clearly. It begins with the risen Lord Jesus appearing to his disciples and saying, "You will receive power when the Holy Spirit comes on you; and you will be my witnesses in Jerusalem, and in all Judea and Samaria, and to the ends of the earth" (Acts 1:8). Every act of the early church is an act that testifies *to* the risen Jesus ascended and ruling. Every act of the early church is also an act *of* the risen Jesus, empowered by him, present by the Spirit, and continuing his earthly ministry through ordinary, weak disciples. Jesus defines and drives it all.

So being located together in Christ is essential. Christ defines us. Only clarity on the single, exclusive gospel of Christ alone can provide a solid basis for unity. We must all be faithful brothers and sisters *in* Christ. However, being also located together in a geographical community is a result of the providential hand of God and a unique opportunity. We are God's holy people *in* Colossae, *in* Birmingham, *in* Barcelona, *in* Brisbane, *in* Boston. And when we share ZIP codes, both spiritual and physical, we discover a common ground, a market square, for collaboration. We aren't rivals of one another but exiles together, called to seek the peace and prosperity of this place (Jeremiah 29:7).

How can churches so different from one another on some doctrinal distinctives and so different in ministry expressions work together fruitfully toward a goal? What do we mean when we talk about sharing a common cause?

Theological Vision

Movements gather around the cause of theological vision. If our core is what we *believe*, and our ministry expressions are what we *do,* then sitting, almost invisibly, somewhere between these two is how we *see*—that is, our theological vision. Vision is how we decide to move from our beliefs to our practice. It's often assumed and unstated, but as we will see, it's a hugely significant component where church collaboration is concerned.

To use a sports analogy, a theological statement provides the rules of the game; ministry expressions are the particular "plays" that spontaneously and dynamically take place on the field. But theological vision is the tactics we employ as we choose our plays. So, theological vision is doctrine filtered and applied to a particular time and place *before* specific ministry expressions are then identified.[5] Michael Felker helpfully explains,

> Theological Vision helps you determine what you are going to do with what you believe within your cultural setting. With a theological vision in place, leaders and churches can make better choices about ministry expressions that are faithful to the Gospel while at the same time are meaningful to their ministry context. That means a greater impact in Worship, Discipleship, Evangelism, Service, and Cultural Engagement.[6]

We live in a complex cultural moment and the church in much of the Western world faces the challenge of existing in a post-Christian society. How do we work out what we will actually do, based on the implications of the gospel? Very often churches and their leaders simply feel their way forward, grappling with issues, suspecting that certain things "won't work" in our world. Whether they could ever put a name to the challenge, they are essentially grappling with theological vision. We know what we believe, we think we know what we ought to do, but we've never really thought about how we got from one to the other. Theological vision is at work quietly enabling us to choose between many potential ministry priorities.

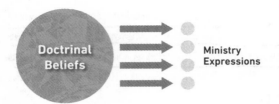

Figure 5.2. Our perception of the relationship between doctrine and practice

Figure 5.2 shows our working perception of the relationship between our doctrinal beliefs and our ministry expressions when we think too simply. We assume that our ministry expressions are pure and universal outworkings of our theology instead of seeing that, in part, they are our attempt to answer the question, "What does it mean for me to be in *Christ* in the *twenty-first century* in *this city*?"

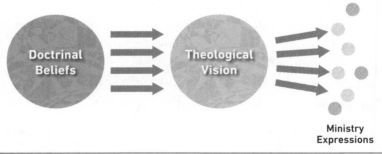

Figure 5.3. The reality of the relationship between doctrine and practice

Figure 5.3 shows the *reality* of the relationship between doctrine and practice. Our ministry expressions aren't universal but are a subset of the options available to us. We have decided on them because we see the world through a particular theological vision. If we operate assuming the first figure is the reality, our theological vision will still be in place but will remain uncontested. That's dangerous, because it may well be that we're operating with a vision that belongs to another time and place, resulting in ministry practices that are outdated or irrelevant. When we understand the role of theological vision, we can ensure it is fit for our purpose, and we can evaluate and adapt our ministry practices to make them more effective.

I (John) have acquired a number of old photographs that chart the early history of the church we helped to revitalize. One picture shows a smartly dressed woman holding a large sign that reads, "Helier Hall Sunday School." Right behind her is a long line of children. When the church was planted in the 1930s, this was the evangelistic strategy for reaching local children. Kids would see the sign and follow it up the hill toward the church. The Sunday school was enormous and ran for many years with remarkable ministry results. I still meet people today, now in their sixties and seventies, who had followed those signs and attended the Sunday school as children.

Why don't we use this strategy today? We still believe the same gospel. We still have a mission to reach children on the housing estate. But if we took that approach, we would likely be viewed with suspicion, perhaps as a Christian equivalent of the pied piper of Hamelin! We do run holiday clubs and youth clubs, and we're involved in school assemblies locally, but our strategies look very different. We seek to engage the whole family and build trust with parents. We recognize that people have changed and times have changed.

Creating a theological vision isn't an attempt to rewrite the gospel for every age; the vision is rooted in our unchanging core but asks how we may meaningfully live out the implications of the gospel in all their fullness in our situation. It's a critical step every generation must take in order to find ways to communicate the gospel clearly and powerfully in the context in which we serve and in contrast to its latest opposites and counterfeits.[7] A sophisticated theological vision was clearly at work in the preaching and life of Paul as he declared, "I have become all things to all people so that by all possible means I might save some" (1 Corinthians 9:22). So, what would it mean for us as a church to be in *Christ*, in the *twenty-first century* in the city of *Birmingham*? Level three partnerships give considerable time to wrestling with these challenges.

Our Time, Our Place

In his book *Center Church*, Tim Keller argues that a good theological vision is found by serious reflection on the themes of "gospel," "city" and "movements." He suggests eight questions through which a theological vision is cultivated and evaluated:

1. What is the gospel, and how do we bring it to bear on the hearts of people today?

2. What is the culture like, and how can we both connect to it and challenge it in our communication?

3. Where are we located—city, suburb, town, rural area—and how does this affect our ministry?

4. To what degree and how should Christians be involved in civic life and cultural production? *"CITY-FYING"*

5. How do the various ministries in the church—word and deed, community and instruction—relate to one another?

6. How innovative will our church be and how traditional?

7. How will our church relate to other churches in our city and region?

8. How will we make our case to the culture about the truth of Christianity?[8]

Allow us to take a moment to attempt to answer those questions in a narrative form for our own contexts.

✝CITY IS A VERB.

Crossway Church. My (John's) church, Crossway, is in a suburb of Birmingham in the middle of a large blue-collar community where the ZIP code is regarded as in the top 8 percent of the most deprived communities in the United Kingdom. There are large numbers of unemployed people, low-paid shift workers in the service industry, and single mothers. There are a number of obvious significant issues, including addiction, domestic violence, debt, mental health problems, and other health issues. The main street is made up of five basic types of shop: bargain stores, charity shops, takeaway food, pawn shops, and betting shops. This affects ministry in a number of important ways.

The gospel, as a gift of eternal salvation and rescue from judgment, always remains the same. Particular implications of the gospel, such as God as Father, freedom from slavery to sin, the possibility of a fresh start and new beginning, and the possibility of change and growth, resonate deeply with people. Many people locally may quickly recognize that they are sinners who may well be facing a judgment to come. They may also have some kind of superstitious belief in God and the supernatural world. It may be harder for them to believe that there is a God who loves them enough to step into the world and save them. And it's a huge challenge to begin to work out the lordship of Jesus in every area of life.

As a church, we have a strategic—and a little dilapidated—building in the heart of the community, and we run a lot of activities from there. People are nervous about going to one another's houses and aren't used to attending evening meetings, but they may be free during the day. Because of irregular shift patterns, attendance of courses, training programs, and regular gatherings is challenging. But people do have time.

One of our key commitments is to raise up indigenous church leaders, and we do a lot of one-on-one and small-group discipleship on an ongoing and ad hoc basis. The ministries of the church are low-key and long-term. We run outreach youth clubs, and there are lots of young people, including eighteen-year-olds whom we met when they were ten and who still live locally with no intention of moving away. Sunday morning is informal, and although the culture isn't one in which people are used to reading, it doesn't follow that they're treated as though they're stupid. We focus on Scripture, and the sermon is usually about forty minutes long, delivered in a conversational style—with a single clear idea running through it and with elements of congregational participation. It's common for the speaker to be interrupted by heckling, for people to wander in and out of the main hall, for things to start late, and for practical aspects of a meeting not to work very well. We prize relationship, trust, and acceptance over and above professionalism.

As we slowly develop a pathway for discipleship from first contact all the way to committed church member, we have to think carefully about how we help people practically as well as spiritually in order to equip them to live with Jesus as Lord. This may be in the form of a debt-relief agency or drug-rehabilitation facility. As a church, we don't offer a lot beyond practical hospitality, but we regard ourselves as a stable family member who aid brothers and sisters in Christ in getting the help they need.

Beyond our local context, we're committed to seeing churches reach these kinds of communities all over the city. Bordering us are three other similar but distinct communities that currently have no obvious gospel witness. We don't have large numbers of young, mobile professionals that we can quickly train and send out, but we're committed to playing our part in seeing churches planted and revitalized among the city's poorest people.

City Church. In my church, I (Neil) recognize that perhaps the biggest challenge for many in our secular city is to believe that "religion" could be the good news they've been waiting to hear. City Church's ministry is largely to young professionals who tend to be profoundly secular. Nevertheless, many wonder about origins, meaning, purpose, and satisfaction.

They are in fact quite likely to ask questions on these topics as one secular person commented, "I look inside for answers but find more questions."

That's why we take a two-step approach to reaching people. If they aren't ready to ask questions about God, we start with questions about themselves and the human condition. Our task Sunday by Sunday is to demonstrate from the Bible that the answer to every one of their questions can be found only in a relationship with the living God. It is, to put it in the language of Dr. Daniel Strange, a case of communicating that all human longings are "subversively fulfilled in the gospel of Jesus Christ."[9]

The gospel is also the good news that God is forming a new community built on Jesus Christ—a place where the world really can be as one. Young professionals are working hard with long hours and little job security, they are often lonely, and they lack real community. We want to be a church where every individual is not only welcomed but also valued and included. Our aim is to be a place where relationships are real, and the community is vibrant.

City Church meets in one of the more affluent areas of our city, where there is little felt need that a local church might help address. However, we do seek to demonstrate concern for the poor and marginalized by working in partnership with the Birmingham City Mission on several projects.

Birmingham, as a result of immigration, is becoming both more religious and more secular at the same time. Fifty-seven percent of Birmingham's under-elevens come from ethnic minority groups.

Our church meets in two congregations. Both are strategically placed near university campuses: one is near the University of Birmingham, and the other, our downtown congregation, meets near two other universities. From the outset, ministry to college students has been very important to us. Insofar as God has enabled us to make disciples, raise up leaders, and plant new churches, much of this is the direct fruit of student ministry.

As a home to many young professionals, healthcare workers, lawyers, accountants, and businesspeople, we are keen that members of the church can live out their faith confidently in the workplace. Our faith and work ministry, is designed to equip younger professionals to live out the gospel in their places of employment. In our monthly Partnership breakfasts, we explore workplace themes and consider how the gospel transforms work.

As a church in a leading urban center we experience a high turnover of people; it's typical to have members with us for a few months, or perhaps a couple of years. So we work hard to ensure that we don't grow a large fringe of occasional attenders. We invest significant time and energy to involve and include all who call City Church their home, including appointing a pastor whose role is to help people along a recognized pathway into church life. We believe that if we're going to be a church rather than merely a service provider or preaching platform, everyone should be part of the community in a meaningful way.

We also try to have multiple entry points into church life by providing different ways for people to connect. For example, we run a twenties ministry to help people make meaningful friendships in the church. We eat lunch together once a month after the morning service. We also offer tea and coffee both before and after the morning service.

City Church's church services follow a traditional pattern, but they aren't liturgical. They have a relatively informal tone and feel. In starting a second downtown congregation two years ago, we decided to adopt a different approach. Second City Church is a café-style congregation. We meet in the tea lounge of one of the flagship churches in the city's center. Our meetings start with coffee and cake around tables of six to eight people. A shorter sermon (twenty-five minutes rather than thirty-five) is always followed by ten minutes of discussion over more coffee and cake. Over the course of our meeting we also have a shorter time of sung worship (fifteen minutes rather than twenty-five). A more relaxed feel "lowers the bar," making these meetings more accessible to the unchurched, and conversation after the sermon invites discussion and debate. We have seen more visitors from outside of the church. And we intend that this congregation in particular will be more ethnically diverse, as will its leadership. We're hopeful for the future despite fifty to sixty years of decline in church involvement in our area.

Our relatively prosperous community doesn't need much practical help. But, as we explored above, there are still real needs—deep needs that only the gospel can address. As our society fragments, loneliness and isolation create social poverty that impacts the wealthy and poor alike. And there's a hunger for truth; there's a need for satisfying answers to the human condition; and there's a growing recognition that materialism has failed to deliver happiness. It takes a lot of work not only to study the biblical text week by week in preparation to preach but also to meaningfully engage with cultural narratives and idols of our age. We want our intellectual rigor to be matched by genuine concern for the individual. Where that's done well, we see people begin to be drawn into the church.

City Church is also committed to gospel partnership. Churches in our city aren't particularly large compared with those in other urban centers. Any church bigger than a hundred people is doing well. That means we feel the need for partnership so we can reach our city for Christ.

Summary. We have taken the time to sketch out our two churches' contexts because as different as they are and as different as the ministry approaches we take are, both of these communities are in Birmingham. Cities are very different within their various neighborhoods and areas, and it takes all kinds of churches to reach all kinds of people. City Church would struggle to reach the community Crossway Church reaches, and Crossway would be unfit to engage in the kind of ministry

City has. However, we share a common cause, as do many other churches scattered across the city, and together we're playing our part in helping to reach everyone.

As we both reflect on Keller's questions, it becomes clear that there is no single or universal way to answer them. A church in a rural context should answer them differently than a church in an urban context. A church in an affluent context should answer them differently than a church in an impoverished context. The ministry expressions of a church in New York City don't work in Manchester, UK. The ministry expressions of fifty years ago don't even work in the same church in the same neighborhood today. This isn't necessarily because a church is being unfaithful, and it certainly isn't because the gospel is no longer the power of God. It is most likely because there is a theological vision at work that's no longer serving its purpose.

The nations of the West have changed markedly over the past forty years—and more quickly than anyone could have imagined. In a time when Christianity has been largely rejected, we need to raise significant questions about how we bring the gospel to the next generation. Missiologist Dr. Stuart Murray identified seven transitions that mark a shift from Christendom to a post-Christendom culture that the church has to come to terms with: from the center to the margins, from majority to minority, from settlers to sojourners, from privilege to plurality, from control to witness, from maintenance to mission, and from institution to movement.[10]

By beginning to understand the place Christians occupy within culture today, we will begin to identify the causes to which we should attach ourselves. Notice Murray's final three present necessities: witness, mission, and movement. Theological vision not only serves individual churches in their mission; it also has a powerful ability to identify causes for collaborative movements.

The Role of Cause Within Collaboration

As we begin to grapple with the implications of the gospel in our time and place, and as we ask questions like the ones above, answers begin to emerge—and at times *shared* answers emerge. As Tim Keller puts it, "Two churches can have different doctrinal frameworks and ministry expressions but the same theological vision—and they will feel like sister ministries. On the other hand, two churches can have similar doctrinal frameworks and ministry expressions, but different theological visions—and they will feel distinct."[11]

Articulated clearly, theological vision aids collaboration, galvanizing all kinds of real, meaningful partnerships. For example, in the United Kingdom, three or four churches may partner to run a Christians Against Poverty debt center. Each church has considered its time and place and, as a result, has arrived at a similar ministry expression that they all can bring about together.

Despite the two very different contexts of Crossway Church and City Church, with their different approaches and different ministry emphases, they both focus on reaching the city as a whole by beginning with collaborative church planting.

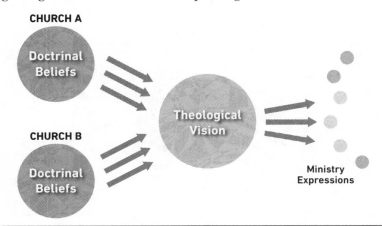

Figure 5.4. Theological vision and collaboration

Figure 5.4 shows how two churches with different doctrinal beliefs share the same theological vision. Although some of their ministry expressions are different, some are the same and can become a cause to collaborate around. So, many of the ministry expressions of Church A are different from Church B's, but because they share the same theological vision for the city, some are the same.

Now think a little bigger. 2020birmingham is not just two churches but a whole room full of church pastors and planters who are making it a priority to gather often to ask the question, "What will it mean for us to be a church in *Christ*, in the *twenty-first century* in this city?" Here we can create together a context to share ideas and insights, establish best practices, develop resources, and offer coaching to those who are starting out or are new to the city. Theological vision creates an incredible opportunity for real, localized movement formation.

Figure 5.5 shows how that works. The driving force behind establishing a cause around which to partner is the theological vision. That

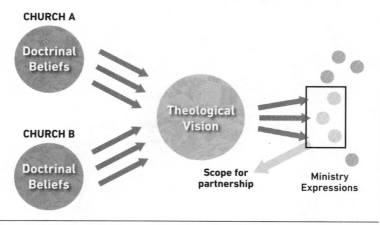

Figure 5.5. Theological vision and level-three partnerships

vision establishes the nature of a church's ministry expressions, and among them a common cause emerges, around which a number of churches with the same vision can begin to coalesce. So theological vision is the glue that holds a movement of diverse churches together. It allows churches to serve a movement rather than simply seek to multiply churches in their own image. The sum is far greater than the parts, and the results are diverse.   *GREATEST AMONG YOU*
                                                                      SERVANT OF ALL

2020birmingham is one local example of a group of churches attempting a level-three partnership. Church planters from a wide variety of networks and denominations express this partnership in their shared concern for the city, their shared desire to learn from one another, and their shared goal of engaging in effective pioneer ministry in the city of Birmingham. Our doctrinal beliefs, while essentially evangelical, are nevertheless somewhat different. Our expressions of ministry within our churches differ to such an extent that we could say we would not feel at home in each other's churches. But the shared theological vision provides the relational glue and drives the partnership toward planting fifty churches by 2030.

As Andy Weatherley, a church planter in the city and our 2020birmingham trainer commented,

> I find that spending time with other 2020 planters is the most energizing gathering of leaders I belong to. Why? Because it is a room full of different people laboring in different contexts but asking the same question: How do we bring the gospel of Christ to this city at this time? This sharpens me for the challenges we are facing in our part of the city. The trust that has grown and the level of honesty on display gets us beyond general theories, into the dirt of real life.

The Cause of Collaboration

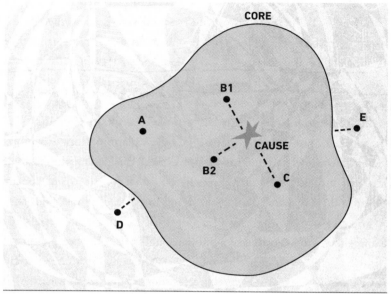

Figure 5.6. The cause of collaboration

Figure 5.6 builds on figure 4.1 at the end of the previous chapter. Not only is the *core* term of the equation in place, functioning as a boundary for the movement, but also the *cause* term. The cause gives fellowship a focus for action. In fact, churches B1 and B2 have found a reason to collaborate with Church C, when previously they had very little to do with each other. With an articulated theological vision, they created space for real collaboration.

In figure 4.1, Church A had close fellowship with churches B1 and B2. It worked closely with the B churches in certain respects, but they didn't share the same theological vision and were therefore yet to see the cause that compels collaboration. In figure 5.6, Church A doesn't yet "get it" and says, "You do your thing, and we'll do ours." Church A is yet to understand the unique contribution of a level-three partnership for the good of the city and the glory of Christ. There is coexistence but not common cause.

Church D may well be onboard with the cause, and it may see highly innovative church-planting strategies as key to growing a church. But because it isn't faithful to the gospel, it still remains outside of the boundary and can't be part of a healthy spiritual movement. The addition of the cause has identified a common answer to the question of what it means to be in Christ at our time and in our place.

So let me (John) tell you about a series of events beginning one Sunday two years ago. A man named Jonggun Lee walked into our morning service with his family. We had never met them before, and after the service Jonggun explained that he was a Korean missionary who had been working with a Korean-speaking church in Birmingham. They had sent him to plant a church that would be best placed to reach international families in which one parent is Korean and the other English. This second generation of Koreans is a growing community in Birmingham, and they're disconnected from the traditional Korean-speaking churches, from which their spouses feel alienated. So this is a harvest field that requires workers.

We talked about the vision he had and the need in the city. He said he was visiting local churches in the few weeks before they began the ministry, adding that I probably wouldn't see him again. I told him about 2020birmingham and how glad I was to meet him. Then we prayed together and said goodbye.

It could have ended there. We could have kept doing our thing, and Jonggun could have gone off and done his. But he and his family returned the next week. Jonggun and his family had so enjoyed the warmth of Crossway, they decided that as they waited to plant, they would stay with us. It was evident that we had connected around a shared core.

Over the following weeks, we learned that not only did we share a core of gospel values, we also shared a cause, and we began to wonder whether we could collaborate with the ministry Jonggun was embarking on. The *core* was enough for us to wish each other well; the *cause* drew us together for this small but unreached group in the city.

Two years in, Jonggun is now a member of our staff at Crossway. We have a fledgling Korean-speaking ministry designed specifically to reach international couples. And we're beginning to see the good news of Jesus shared with the group Jonggun had identified. Both North and South Koreans and their spouses are meeting regularly to read the Bible with Jonggun, and we're working out the next-best step together.

Of course, this ministry was beyond me. My Korean language skills are nonexistent, but Jonggun recognized the value of collaboration. He explained that the Crossway church family "understood each of our differences, but that just helped us be united even more. The enthusiasm to understand international people and their particular pastoral difficulties shown by the elders and members was the main reason that helped us get established with Crossway Church."

I (John) asked Jonggun what helps us work together. He said it was sharing the same core and the same cause. "I believe we can work together well because we have only one goal, which is to serve Christ. . . . Furthermore, it is clear that you care, not only for the Korean group, but also for the international groups that are yet to come." It's amazing how far you can get together with a shared love of Christ and of lost people.

So the *cause* identifies the common answer. But within the formula, the cause has not yet energized movement into actual collaborative action. It has the potential to be a talking point only. For real collaboration to develop, there must be a third additive to the formula. This is the *code*, the DNA that catalyzes the movement, which is the subject of the next chapter.

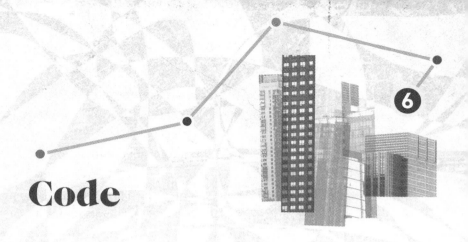

Code

Give me one hundred preachers who fear nothing but sin, and desire nothing but God, and I care not a straw whether they be clergymen or laymen; such alone will shake the gates of hell and set up the kingdom of heaven on earth.

JOHN WESLEY

This chapter is about the third term of the equation for collaboration: a shared code. It covers:

- *how the common code, or DNA, of a movement energizes it for action;*
- *how the code of a movement consists of a contextualized version of the foundational principles that create a bigger vision; and*
- *how within the typology of movement sets, the three terms of the equation—core, cause, and code—make collaborative movements well-formed centered sets.*

So far in part two of this book, we've seen the importance of the terms *core* and *cause* in the equation that creates collaboration. The *core* is a shared set of core beliefs rooted in the gospel that acts as a boundary for the movement. The *cause* is the reason to collaborate, the focus for unity, the particular ministry goal that is your shared answer to what it means to be in Christ in the city in the twenty-first century. The *cause* gives the movement purpose. But what gives the movement its energy and life? What makes a movement *move*? The code.

Neil and I (John) may be united by a core belief in the nutritional value of toast. We may also have discovered that we both believe that the best way to make toast is with a toaster. We may have found what we believe is the best toaster, and we may be dreaming of making toast together. We have the core and the cause in place. But we won't get toast from a toaster unless we plug it in and switch it on.

Turning the toaster people from an interest group into a self-sustaining collaborative movement—this is the *code*. Think of the source code of a computer program, which when executed brings the computer to life and enables it to perform the function for which it was built. Think of genetic code, which provides the instructions for the growth, development, and reproduction of a living organism. Alan Hirsch suggests that "movements are essentially DNA-based organizations."[1]

In this chapter, our focus is not on the specific DNA codes that energize our particular churches but on the shared code across churches that execute a collaborative movement. As planters meet to train, as we gather each month for the forum, as we cast a vision for the city, as we pray together, and as we deal with all of the content in the annual conference, we're trying to celebrate this code and not merely assume or even undermine it.

It's tempting at this point to think purely in terms of strategy and to focus on learning how businesses get things done. But the true life-giver of a movement must be the Lord Jesus Christ. For anything healthy to happen, we need to be plugged into him.

So, in what sense is the *code* really any different from the *core*? We've learned that a shared set of *core* beliefs rooted in the gospel brings trust, respect, and mutual appreciation, but it isn't enough on its own to get collaboration going. Given the foundation (core) and given the focus (cause), you also need fuel (code). This catalyzing ingredient gets you moving down the road.

But having said that this ingredient is not simply the shared set of *core* beliefs, rooted in the gospel, we must also be careful that we don't detach it from the gospel. The gospel is the way *in*, and the gospel must be the way *on*. There is a danger in collaboration that the minute we want to start seeing results, we forget the very thing that brought us together in the first place: the gospel.

Tightrope walker Charles Blondin (1824–1897) set up a rope across Niagara Falls and walked across it both forward and backward. Then he performed tricks, including sitting on a stool on the wire and eating a meal. Then he asked for a volunteer. Would anyone allow him to carry them across the falls, along the wire, on his back? What trust it would take to allow oneself to be carried across on that man's shoulders!

Now suppose that, halfway across, the volunteer leaned down and said to Blondin, "Thanks for getting me this far, but I'm not sure I trust you anymore. I think I'll walk from here." Blondin's reply would probably not be repeatable. What would the rider's family and friends say? What would you say to that rider?[2]

Could it be that we're tempted to behave just like that volunteer when it comes to church-planting movements? We gather because of a gospel of grace, but very soon we want to get going—to see results. We want to realize the vision on our own and in our own strength. Paul wrote, "Are you so foolish? After beginning by means of the

Spirit, are you now trying to finish by means of the flesh?" (Galatians 3:3). "Don't be crazy!" he seemed to be crying.

So when we consider the equation that energizes the movement, we need to be careful not to stray from God's grace and to turn to human wisdom, strategy, ingenuity, and strength. In 2020birmingham, we've developed a DNA code that flows out of the five implications of the gospel that create a bigger vision outlined in part one of this book: fidelity, urgency, compassion, generosity, and humility. These are convictions that lead us into a box-C vision.

The DNA code takes these five implications of the gospel and works them out for each context. So 2020birmingham's code is simply fidelity, urgency, compassion, generosity, and humility translated into postures that we seek to adopt toward one another, the task of planting, and our city.

2020birmingham's DNA

The following code is what energizes all that we do at 2020birmingham. It's our culture. Initially it was implicit within the group; it was caught more than taught. Because of the highly relational origin of 2020birmingham, the code hasn't been formalized as a document or a statement that members have been required to sign. Like real biological DNA, the code isn't written in bold. However, early in conversation, this DNA was communicated, and throughout all that takes place, it is explicitly taught and implicitly reinforced as well as celebrated.

At times, a group interested in understanding 2020birmingham tries to work out how to partner with us. They clearly share the same core convictions in relation to the gospel. They clearly share the same cause to see the whole city renewed by the gospel. However, they struggle to identify with elements of the code, perhaps because of their aversion to collaboration or because they aren't persuaded that church planting is going to be key to seeing communities reached for Jesus. We suggest that a shared code is just as important as a shared core and cause.

We've told the story of 2020birmingham many times to leaders of different networks and denominations. Many have been enthusiastic about our collaborative approach to planting—but not all. Some have expressed concern about working across a broad range of evangelical churches. One church planter is flourishing within a level-two partnership. But he made it clear that he was very nervous that level-three movements were inherently unstable because growth is at the expense of faithfulness to the gospel. He recognized that level-three movements risk broadening too quickly. The push for growth could be at the cost of a commitment to the gospel.

We've found it difficult to understand why some people aren't ready to embrace a vision for working together to reach a city. After all, what faithful church would not want to do whatever it takes to reach lost people? And why wouldn't we lock arms with those we believe are also laboring in the Lord? We wonder, *Don't they care enough?* But this isn't a generous way to approach others' questions!

A possible answer came into view when clinical psychologist Dr. Jordan B. Peterson introduced me (Neil) to the problem of optimization.[3] He described situations in which being effective in reaching a goal isn't always about choosing between two factors (in our case choosing between fidelity and generosity), rather it's often a case of deciding which of two necessary factors matter most. In certain situations, "two or more factors are important, but one cannot be maximized without diminishing the others," Peterson writes.[4] He suggests cooperation and competition as examples. We both want and need to cooperate with others (providing us with security and stability), yet we also want to compete against others (so we can get ahead). This is the problem of optimization we love to see at play on TV shows like *The Apprentice* when individuals compete to win the prize but must collaborate in order to avoid being fired.

Although it may be easier to paint a group of churches as "not getting it," if we all agree the need is urgent, we all want optimization. Everyone would agree that faithfulness and generosity are important, but how do we affirm them and arrange them in such a way that we achieve maximization? The problem for all of us is the problem of optimization. In our desire to maximize one factor, we must diminish the others.

This is fundamentally a *code* issue. The DNA we establish determines how we seek to achieve optimization. The code doesn't simply affirm values that would be shared by many other networks; it also celebrates the factors we're maximizing so we reach the goal we set.

One conversation I (Neil) had with a level-two leader helped me to understand his concern. He felt nervous at the thought of pursuing growth at almost any cost. Level-three movements have a degree of unpredictability and instability built into their very structure. You don't quite know who will walk into the room, and if you attempt to grow too quickly, you may grow at the expense of the core.

This same leader was willing to work with certain other denominations. Some of the churches he had helped to plant belonged to more than one conservative-reformed network. He commented, "Lots of our churches are multibadged because we recognize that a single network can't provide everything." But his commitment to staying at level two was clear. "We tend to look for partnerships with theologically similar organizations. In local cooperation, we've limited the breadth with our Doctrinal Statement of Faith."

We agree that committing church planters to level-three relationships exposes them to other voices and influences. One network won't share the same vision and values or the same position on secondary matters of doctrine as another. That introduces risk, but as we've already argued, it also introduces synergy.

My (Neil's) friend, the level-two leader, wisely pointed out,

> The key question is, What is entailed by collaboration? It is one thing to run a conference together. It is another to provide church-planter training. It is one thing to provide a listening ear to a case study presentation and then critique. It is another to cooperate in church-planter selection. I think the principle of "greater collaboration requiring greater agreement" holds fast.

We agree with this point and maintain that there is still a way for us to be "together, planting churches" in a way that harnesses the extraordinary strength of cross-tribal collaboration, as opposed to "planting churches together" without due regard for our differences.

However, when it comes to optimization, it's clear where my friend stands. The DNA code of his network leads him to this conclusion:

> We want everyone in our church-planting network to be able to wholeheartedly and unreservedly commend the gospel ministry of all our church plants. That's got to be the case if we're encouraging people to leave one church and join the launch team of another. If I'm being brutally honest, that's probably an aspiration rather than a reality. But, in theory, it ought to be possible. I want each of our planted churches to pass the "Would I be happy if my kids went there?" test. I'm not really interested in pouring my energies into planting churches that won't reflect my theological convictions.

We must acknowledge the wisdom of what is being said here. We also must have confidence in the church-planting movement we're seeking to cultivate. However, our argument so far has been that, as churches, we can continue to function at level one and level two, but fidelity, urgency, compassion, generosity, and humility together compel us to function at level three as well.

We have different codes for different contexts. As churches we are more than capable of functioning at all three levels at the same time. I (Neil) find time in the week to meet with my fellow FIEC pastors and when I do I'm functioning at level 1. On another occasion I will be part of a local preaching group with other like-minded evangelicals who share a conviction for expository preaching. When I'm there I'm enjoying level 2 fellowship. Then later in the day I'm with my fellow 2020birmingham planters, level 3. At different levels our partnerships are programmed to achieve optimization in different ways. Moving between them becomes second nature after a while.

Many churches that belong to 2020birmingham also belong to tighter networks that prize a high level of doctrinal clarity on secondary matters; this diminishes their ability to be generous at that level. The movement 2020birmingham is seeking to be simply affords them a second context with a second code for the sake of the city. We should be able to have our cake and eat it too!

In fact, we want to suggest that operating at both level two *and* three is the best way to achieve true optimization. Our argument throughout this chapter is that this code—the DNA of 2020birmingham—is an essential and complementary code if churches are really going to respond to the urgent need to be together for the city, with all its complexity and in all its diversity. To be blunt, as a white conservative-evangelical church planter in Birmingham, operating among the ruins of Christendom, I need all the help I can get!

Code 1: Jesus Is Lord and the Local Church Is the Hope for the World

This first line of code flows out of the principle of fidelity outlined in chapter one. The Lord Jesus Christ came into the world to seek and save the lost. Through his death on the cross, he has come to rescue sinners like you and me from the just, eternal punishment of a holy God. In his resurrection and ascension, Jesus is enthroned and rules over the entire world. He will one day return to judge the living and the dead. This means that today is the day of salvation, and we are saved through repentance and faith.

For every believer in every age, the mission is simple: "go and make disciples" (Matthew 28:19). We are not seeking simply to serve the city or bring justice, though those are implications of our mission. We aren't seeking simply to meet the presenting needs of those we're trying to reach. We are seeking to call people to a new fidelity to King Jesus. In his book *Turning to God,* David Wells wrote,

> The gospel is not first and foremost about us. It is not a device for getting what we want or need. It is not a technique for self-improvement or self-accomplishment. It is not a means of tapping our own inner resources. It does not offer itself as a tool for thinking positively about ourselves. It is not about us at all, although we are invited to believe its message. It is about Christ. It is about the actions of the triune God as he reaches out to sinners who can neither save themselves nor bow before him in submission apart from the working of his grace (Rom 8:6-8).[5]

Though the city of Birmingham is a complicated place made up of rich and poor, young and old, religiously devout and ardent secularist, powerful and powerless from every corner of the earth, the foundational principle is that the death and resurrection of Jesus has identified him as the global Lord, and God is drawing sinners to bow the knee before him. It isn't about us, but about him. If the gospel compels fidelity to Christ for the Ethiopian eunuch of Acts 8 and the slave girl of Acts 16, then it also compels fidelity to Christ for the Athenian philosophers of Acts 17 and the king and his wife of Acts 26. As Paul said to King Agrippa concerning the gospel message, "I stand here and testify to small and great alike" (Acts 26:22).

The gospel is the solution to our plight, and God has ordained that it be embodied within the glory of the local church. The church is Christ's body and Christ's bride. Ephesians 2 and 3 make it clear that new life in Christ and new friendship with God and others result in a new family of God in which he lives by his Spirit (Ephesians 2:22). And the church is therefore the center of God's plan to display his manifold wisdom to the entire cosmos (3:10). In Paul's correspondence with Timothy and Titus as he approached the end of his life, the health of local churches is at the forefront of his mind. As Tim Chester wrote, "The overriding passion of the first-century believers was to be church in a way that kept the gospel central for life, growth, and mission."[6]

Consider the words of Jesus: "A new command I give you: Love one another. As I have loved you, so you must love one another. By this everyone will know that you are my disciples, if you love one another" (John 13:34-35). Where is this love displayed? In the local church! In his book *9 Marks of a Healthy Church* Mark Dever concluded, "The local church is God's evangelism plan. The local church is God's evangelism program."[7]

When we look at the complex challenges of a city like Birmingham—the sociological headaches and the economic black holes—it may be tempting to want to rewrite the book and convince ourselves that churches, as helpful as they may have been in the past, are simply inadequate for the twenty-first century. Churches are weak, messy, flawed, derided, and unimpressive. Ask anyone in the city center of Birmingham, "What does this city need?" and no one will answer, "More churches!"

But the command of Jesus, "the life of Paul, and the action of the early church demonstrate that church planting was a primary activity. Any church wishing to rediscover the dynamic nature of the early church should consider planting new churches."[8] Why? Because the local church embodies the true hope for the world. In fact, Keller argued that

the vigorous, continual planting of new congregations is the single most crucial strategy for (1) the numerical growth of the body of Christ in any city, and (2) the continual corporate renewal and revival of the existing churches in a city. Nothing else—not crusades, outreach programs, para-church ministries, growing mega-churches, congregational consulting, nor church renewal process—will have the consistent impact of dynamic, extensive church planting.[9]

In a US context, authors Ed Stetzer and Warren Bird note,

Among *established* Southern Baptist churches, for example, there are 3.4 baptisms per one hundred resident members, but their *new* churches average 11.7. That's more than three times more! Other denominations offer similar numbers. It's not hard to conclude that the launching of more new churches will lead more people to Christ.[10]

Further evidence would support this claim. In 2017 the North American Mission Board reported that in Canada 71 percent of all baptisms happened through churches started since 2010. In Wisconsin, more baptisms came from church plants than from all other Southern Baptist Convention churches combined. In the New England states, 24 percent of all baptisms were through church plants.[11]

If more people are to come under the lordship of Jesus, what is needed is a greater commitment to planting. Our prayer is that it may be possible for every faithful church in Birmingham to be able to affirm three statements:

1. If we could, we would plant churches.

2. Therefore when we can, we will plant churches.

3. In the meantime, we will do what we can to help others plant churches.

We are united by a desire not just to see people blessed or impacted or encouraged or helped but to see them graciously, gloriously converted and beginning to follow Jesus, playing their part in his Great Commission. And the simple biblical reality is that disciples are made primarily through the planting of churches.

Listen to the reflections of one Birmingham pastor, Colin Tamplin, who has taken his church on something of a journey toward sharing the 2020birmingham code:

> Some pastors are known as "church-planting pastors" and their churches as "church-planting churches." They have made church planting the goal of their whole existence, and all their ministries are directed toward it. But what if neither you nor your church could be so described? How can church planting nevertheless remain on your agenda, and how can you be readied to respond when an opportunity does arise?
>
> In my case, the answer has been 2020birmingham. For over twenty years I led a medium-to-large congregation in the south of Birmingham that would not be described as an "intentionally church-planting" church. We had been absorbed for many years in establishing our presence on a new housing estate and then engaging in a major development of the inadequate

premises we had inherited. Church planting was not prominent on our agenda.

But at the same time I became involved with 2020birmingham, having been invited to be part of its initial steering group. I met eager church planters and heard of the ways in which churches were working together to see churches planted in the city. It was clear that a movement was being created that would enable churches to do far more together, and more strategically, than they ever would on their own.

And then in 2016 an opportunity arose for our church to be involved in a very significant church revitalization project. A local pastor contacted me about his concern that his church needed a deliberate plan to support the enthusiastic but elderly congregation if they were to survive more than a few more years. 2020birmingham was the obvious place to turn. To cut a long story short, with 2020birmingham as a catalyst we were able to raise the matter with the congregation, introduce them to a prospective new leader, encourage them with stories from another local revitalized church and finally transfer a core group of eight from three nearby churches, including an elder and his family from my own. Today the church is settling into the new phase of its life, with the faithful old and enthusiastic new growing and reaching out together.

It is impossible to think that this could have happened without 2020birmingham. There would not have been the expertise, the cooperation, or the trust for this to happen. And having seen this work out in practice has given our church a confidence that we could be used in even greater ways in the future if God should so call us.

So our prayer is that church leaders across the city will share Tim Keller's sentiment and "think of church planting as just one of the things the church does along with everything else. . . . Planting should be as much an ongoing, natural part of your ministry as worship, evangelism, fellowship, education, and service."[12] When a critical number of churches in any one place share the conviction that new churches are necessary to reach our communities with the gospel, a movement is born.

Code 2: Our City Is Lost, and We Can't Reach It on Our Own

The second code is simply a contextualized version of the principle of urgency, also outlined in chapter one. In the United Kingdom, one church in every 150 will die each year.[13] The Church of England closes a church every ten days, on average.[14] Church planting is going on; in fact, six new churches open somewhere in England every week and have been for thirty years.[15] But we aren't even standing still in terms of numbers. Across the United Kingdom, there was a net loss of six hundred churches over the last five years.[16] In the West Midlands (where Birmingham is located), among the mainline denominations the closure rate is at its highest.[17]

This should not surprise us, as over the next couple of years, Sunday church attendance in our region is predicted to drop to 3.8 percent. The figure for Bible-believing evangelicals is significantly lower than that and is supported by population migration as Christians from other countries make their home in our city. In an urban context, church transfer is common and gives the illusion of growth, but it's akin to the rearranging of furniture on a sinking ship. Many of the churches that belong to 2020birmingham are experiencing modest growth through conversion, but among them a high proportion of these converts are "prodigals" returning to a faith. Our city remains unreached.

When we look around us, things look complex: the demographic challenges, the socioeconomic struggles, competing methodologies, and the latest research. What does wisdom look like? How do we make the most of our opportunity in our time and for our context?

Churchill wrote, "Out of intense complexities, intense simplicities emerge."[18] If heaven and hell are real, if our cities are full of lost people, if the gospel is the hope for the world, then our task is obvious. This glorious, simple gospel of God is good news for every person in every community, from every tribe, nation, and tongue, living in every corner of the unreached world, including the city of Birmingham. It sounds easy, but three things make heralding this gospel hard.

First, it's hard because the gospel message needs to be *carried with care*. It requires faithful workers who will go into the harvest field, who will deny themselves, take up their cross, and follow Jesus into obscure or dangerous areas, carefully carrying the gospel with them.

Second, the task is hard because the message needs to be *communicated with clarity*. It requires faithful workers who will work hard at conveying this good news in word and action, in a way that's intelligible to both the speaker and the hearer. Each of us is thankful that we have the Word of God in a language we understand. Are we doing the work of translation for those we are seeking to reach? That's what reaching a city like Birmingham requires.

Third, the task is hard because it is entirely *contingent on Christ*. People don't just need new information; they need new life. Actually, this makes the task impossible! Elijah prayed, "Answer me, LORD, answer me, so these people will know that you, LORD, are God, and that you are turning their hearts back again" (1 Kings 18:37). Only God can turn our hearts back to him.

But as hard as it may be, the task is also urgent. We must stop seeing the city as simply a powerhouse for profit and progress or a center of excellence and influence. We must start to see it as communities of lost people who are without hope and without God in the world, who desperately need to be rescued from the dominion of darkness and brought into the kingdom of Jesus. If we do, it will drive us to our knees and humble us to see that no single church, network, or denomination could possibly accomplish this task alone.

Pulsing through 2020birmingham's veins is a recognition of the need and of the imperative of a commitment to respond collaboratively. That's deeply attractive to church planters. Jez Dearing was one of the first planters with 2020birmingham, planting Oikos Church in 2010. He contributes in numerous ways to the movement, and the church is currently preparing to plant again. He reflected,

> 2020birmingham is a credible response to the need to see our city renewed by the gospel. We desire new disciples, we need disciples who make disciples, we need churches of disciples who will plant new churches in every area of our city, particularly among the hard-to-reach areas and peoples. Personally, what I appreciate about 2020 is the generous spirit among the different churches in working together, and the breath of wisdom and experience around church which we can all call upon.

The spiritual need of the city of Birmingham requires us to stretch what we believe is possible and to "look outside the standard toolbox of solutions."[19] Hardwired into our code is a commitment to collaborate, because we know that what we're attempting to do, we can't achieve on our own.

It has been said that "the only actions that become springboards to succeeding big are those informed by big thinking to begin with."[20] To use the terminology we've been developing in the book, box-C thinking compels us toward level-three partnership from the outset. When the vision is to reach a city, the method must involve collaboration.

Code 3: There Is No Favoritism in God's Kingdom

The third line of code is the outworking of the principle of compassion (outlined in chapter one). Although the marks of a healthy church remain a constant biblical norm, there is no "one size fits all" when it comes to how churches reflect their people and their context. We recognize that the boundaries of geography, economics, class, ethnicity, and language create challenges that are not easily overcome without considerable intentionality. If we are going to truly reach our city in all its diversity, we need to humbly acknowledge our limitations and seek to act without prejudice to enable the planting of churches that *can do* what our present churches *can't do* on their own. Sometimes we approach the concept of church multiplication as though it is duplication, but that causes us to continue to reach the same kinds of people. The challenge is to attempt the kind of multiplication that results in churches that are qualitatively and strategically different.

Four times in the New Testament, we're told that God does not show favoritism (Acts 10:34; Romans 2:11; Galatians 2:6; Ephesians 6:9). As a result, three times we're told not to show favoritism ourselves (1 Timothy 5:21; James 2:1, 9). This passage from the book of James is particularly convicting on this issue:

> Suppose a man comes into your meeting wearing a gold ring and fine clothes, and a poor man in filthy old clothes also comes in. If you show special attention to the man wearing fine clothes and say, "Here's a good seat for you," but say to the poor man, "You stand there" or "Sit on the floor by my feet," have you not discriminated among yourselves and become judges with evil thoughts?
>
> Listen, my dear brothers and sisters: Has not God chosen those who are poor in the eyes of the world to be rich in faith and to inherit the kingdom he promised those who love him? (James 2:2-5)

Within the context of a single church, this kind of favoritism may stand out; however, it is less obvious when it comes to the actions of a church-planting movement. But we must not be naive. The stark reality is that wealthy, white, middle-class people tend to plant wealthy, white, middle-class churches. If the vision is only to plant churches on an occasional or ad-hoc basis, there will be a bias toward the kind of favoritism that the New Testament roundly condemns.

For a city like Birmingham, more than twenty new congregations will be needed. The number is probably closer to one hundred among every kind of community our city holds. It's tempting to be drawn only toward plants that we know will "work" and will become viable quickly. It's tempting to be drawn toward contexts that seem easier rather than toward those that are apparently impenetrable. It's tempting to reach only for the low-hanging fruit. If we do so, large swathes of our city will be left shrouded in darkness.

Comprehensive church planting requires more effort than simply finding the quickest and easiest way to reach a numerical goal. It requires prayer, thought, care, and money to ensure we're seeking to plant among our poorest, most marginalized, and apparently least "reachable" people groups. Compassion means being committed to exposing our unconscious biases, resisting favoritism, and planting without prejudice. To return to the early church for a moment, Eckhard Schnabel reflects on the missionary tactics of Paul:

> The basic rule of missionary work is, for Paul, the consistent commitment to the listener, whom he takes very seriously. Jews need to be reached with the gospel as Jews, and likewise Gentiles as Gentiles. The one decisive factor is that people are won for faith in Jesus Christ (1 Cor 9:19). This basic rule controls Paul's behavior: he can live as a Jew among Jews, and he can live like a Gentile among Gentiles (1 Cor 9:20). Paul's behavior reflects his

conviction that all people need to hear the gospel: the elites of the Greco-Roman world in the cities as well as uncultured bar-barians, the educated and the ignorant (Rom 11:14). . . . Paul is never content with existing missionary "successes," nor does he give up when only a few people are converted: he constantly strives to reach more people with the message of Jesus Christ (1 Cor 9:19; Rom 10:18), and he never gives up hope that more Gentiles, and more Jews (Rom 10:16), will come to faith in Jesus Christ.[21]

For us, there's still a lot of work to do in this area. We haven't thought strategically enough to have a top-ten list of where we want to plant churches. As you've read the story of 2020birmingham, you may have noticed that, though there's increasing diversity, there's cer-tainly a higher proportion of newly planted churches among white middle-class people. If you were to view the plants on a map, you would see that the eastern part of the city, which is the poorest and most ethnically diverse, is underserved in comparison to other areas. Initially, we were simply excited to see something happening, but as we grow up, we're seeking to have a strategy that avoids the uncon-scious favoritism we've seen in the early years.

But it won't just be strategy that does it. I (John) was recently talking to someone who arrived as an asylum seeker in the city through the ministry of one 2020birmingham church. He was a church planter in his native country, and because the local imam had been converted, a fatwa had been pronounced on this individual. So he was in our city, and by the providential hand of God was just the person to reach a community that would be way beyond most of us. God had given him a clear vision to plant a church for the least-reached people in our city, which included a vision to raise up indigenous leaders for the long term. Why did he think 2020birmingham was the right context for him? Because he saw it as the best platform for support, collaboration, and a united response by the churches of Birmingham.

Code 4: The More Generous We Are, the More Fruitful We Will Be

The fourth line of code is a reinforcement of the principle of generosity outlined in chapter one. The biblical paradox is that the more we give away, the greater the gain for the gospel. Jesus said, "Give, and it will be given to you. A good measure, pressed down, shaken together and running over, will be poured into your lap. For with the measure you use, it will be measured to you" (Luke 6:37-38). Sadly, this verse has often been appropriated by proponents of the prosperity gospel in ways that undermine God's grace and prey on vulnerable people, and you may have been tempted to use it yourself at your church's latest finance meeting. But let's not lose sight of what's actually being said. J. C. Ryle unpacks it for us: "No man shall ever be the loser, in the long run, by deeds of self-denying charity, and patient long-suffering love."[22]

When Paul encouraged the Corinthian church to join with the Macedonian churches in giving financial support to the church in Jerusalem, he said, "Remember this: Whoever sows sparingly will also reap sparingly, and whoever sows generously will also reap generously" (2 Corinthians 9:6). No doubt the church in Jerusalem was very different from the one in Corinth. But neither was impeccable (as is evident 1 Corinthians and Galatians). There would have been many persuasive reasons for them to keep their wallets closed tight. But they were called to be generous, and it was good for them to be.

For 2020birmingham, this means we're convinced that the more generous we are toward one another, the more fruitful we'll be in our mission to reach the city. It isn't that our networks, denominations, and secondary theological concerns aren't important. We all land where we do because of heartfelt convictions. But they rightly take second place to a fundamental unity in Christ that means we rejoice in the fruit of each other's ministries. We aren't engaged in the kingdom work of a single church, a single network, or even a single movement like 2020birmingham; we are engaged in the kingdom work of God.

The corollary of this is that "from the one who has been entrusted with much, much more will be asked" (Luke 12:48). The opportunity to be generous is also a responsibility. Where we've been blessed with money, workers, opportunities, skills, resources, and experience, we are called to pass on what we can to whoever we can for the cause of the gospel. We must continually guard against quietly wishing someone would stop "because he was not one of us" (Mark 9:38) and to do what we can to be generous.

Within 2020birmingham that means the most unlikely churches give financially to each other. Churches that have previously had very little to do with each other regularly pray for each other. Where it's appropriate, churches encourage their members to join the core teams of plants that aren't directly affiliated to them, perhaps because they live in the area being reached, have a calling to that community, or have a gift set that's needed. When an opportunity in the city is identified, we work together to find the best solution, regardless of the final form of the church plant. Most months our planters forum has visitors and guests who are welcome to come and receive anything of value. Someone planting outside the movement isn't a threat or regarded with suspicion but someone we invite to talk and we offer help to. We're convinced that the more we give away, the more we gain.

Generosity takes many forms. Barnaby Pain, a church planter with 2020birmingham who is one year into a church revitalization project, makes this clear. He emailed the following to me (John) recently, when I asked him to reflect on why he planted with 2020birmingham.

I felt, since Bible college, that the only place I could lead a revital-ization would be in Birmingham. Why? I knew revitalization would mean a lot of challenges. I knew I was not some amazing rugged hero with vast experience who could accomplish change alone. I felt weak and unimpressive, and facing up to my own limitations and weakness meant that leading a revitalization would require more than just me and my young family.

So we needed the generous support of faithful people with us and the support of faithful pastors around us. Birmingham was the only place I thought we had this, and we had it there in abundance!

We were able to gather a first-class team of families to join with us to kick-start the revitalization. The benefit of collabor-ative church planting and the thriving movement of church planting in Birmingham was that all these people already knew what was expected; they'd seen it done. And churches were willing to be generous in giving us their best.

Another benefit is the ongoing partnership between churches. Just because we took a group of families a year and three months ago does not in any sense mean the job is done. Ongoing needs arise at different stages of our journey, and the churches around us get this. They are in constant contact to pray and offer real practical support.

I just had a conversation today with the pastor of a partner church. We were the first plant they had ever sent people to. They are now thinking how they can be further involved in planting or revitalization in the city. Will they plant them-selves? Will they send a second wave of people to ensure our revitalization is stabilized at a tricky time when people are feeling tired? We shared our struggles honestly, and due to our partnership we can work together in very practical ways to help both our churches thrive.

As a revitalization one year in, we don't have people power and we don't have much time, but God has blessed our members with generosity. Because we belong to 2020birmingham, we knew another recent church plant was struggling financially, so as part of our gift day we set aside a substantial amount of money to support them. It was such a thrill for us to partner in real ways with another local plant, to give when we had been given so much ourselves.

Barnaby and the rest of this young church revitalization project get the code.

Code 5: Somehow We Are Stronger Together

The fifth line of code applies to the principle of humility, outlined in chapter one. It isn't uncommon for young church planters reaching out for help to be told that going solo is good for them. The old weather-beaten planter may reminisce, "Struggling for survival on your own is the thing that will humble you and shape you. That's how we did it! We had nothing and no one, and we all nearly died, but against all odds the church was established." The picture of the lone-ranger, hairy-chested, Elijah type, one man on a mission to reach the world, has historically been the church-planter model.

Praise God that he graciously works through individuals in this way, but one recent piece of research concluded, "The likelihood of church survivability increases by 135 percent when the church planter meets at least monthly with a group of church planting peers."[23] We are stronger together. And we are healthier together. Business writer

Patrick Lencioni notes, "Peer-to-peer accountability is the primary and most effective source of accountability on the leadership team of a healthy organization."[24] Of course this makes perfect sense. If a context has been created in which church planters with a common core, cause, and code can gather to encourage, support, and equip one another, only good will come of it.

One author looking at research on elite performance observed, "The single most important difference between these amateurs and the three groups of elite performers is that the future elite performers seek out teachers and coaches and engage in supervised training, whereas the amateurs rarely engage in similar types of practice." He concluded, "No one succeeds alone and no one fails alone. Pay attention to the people around you."[25] For 2020birmingham, collaboration is not just a necessary evil that we must reluctantly engage in because it's the only way we'll reach the city; it's a wonderful opportunity that by God's grace produces stronger, healthier churches.

Listen to Barnaby again:

> I receive 1-2-1 coaching from John, who is much further down the revitalization road than us. He enabled us to set realistic expectations for our first year. We weren't gung-ho, thinking we would change the world, but we weren't venturing out into unknown territory either. Our expectations were real. And so a year in, when asked, "How's it going?" we could honestly say "Actually, as expected."
>
> Another amazing benefit is the ongoing peer-to-peer support of our planters forum, where we meet monthly for prayer, encouragement, correction, and training. I look forward to this gathering every month, where there's a real band-of-brothers feeling. This lifts us out of our isolated silos to celebrate God's work across the city and to bring our needs before him and one another. Without

this monthly gathering, planting would be lonely and wearisome; yet here are brothers and sisters who have been through it, who can speak much needed gospel wisdom into my heart.

Synergy is important as we learn from each other in unexpected ways. There are strategic advantages when different groups with different emphases and different gifts gather for a common cause. But the outcome of the collaboration and the route toward the goal may not have been identified before the journey began. The right steps aren't always obvious, and only as we come together with the same heart and the same burden does clarity begin.

This is attractive to people considering partnering with the 2020birmingham. Individuals involved in a church plant—from a sending church, as a planter, or as part of a core team—can believe church planting is possible for them rather than only the domain of an elite group of super-Christians. When they face a huge task *together*, attitudes of "it won't work" can quickly become "we will each play our parts because we aren't on our own."

This may begin slowly. Trust and understanding take time but are crucial ingredients if others will be drawn in. Spiritual, ecclesial, and missional credibility must be demonstrated, and a tentative beginning may give time for partnerships to coalesce before they then pick up the pace. In 2020birmingham, group leaders seek to envision new partners all the time. There's a huge time commitment in collaboration, which can often feel like a luxury—or at least less urgent than everything else that needs to be done. In the end, only a deep conviction that somehow we are stronger together makes collaboration a priority well before any measurable results.

Over time, such collaboration leads to endurance among those planting. With 2020birmingham, Jonny Richards planted the Gate Church in 2014. He reflects on his experience:

Church planting was once described to me as being like flying a plane while you are still building it. That makes for a pretty bumpy ride at times, and on occasion I have wondered if I could go on. Through 2020birmingham I have been blessed with regular contact and support from men and women who well know the toils but have also experienced over and over that Christ's grace is sufficient. Time and again they have been his means of grace to me—offering ongoing coaching, wise advice, empathetic listening, prayerful support, and kind humor that helps me regain perspective and the strength to press on.

Bounded-Set and Center-Set Movements

So, the five lines of code cohere and energize 2020birmingham:

1. Jesus is Lord, and the local church is the hope for the world.

2. Our city is lost, and we can't reach it on our own.

3. There is no favoritism in God's kingdom.

4. The more generous we are, the more fruitful we will be.

5. Somehow we are stronger together.

Wherever you slice us, this is what we bleed! Now that we can see these in action, it's helpful to understand a little more about the nature of the movement we're advocating. It's common in conversations about missiology to speak of the difference between bounded-set and centered-set groups. For some, a bounded set is an essential way to establish who is "in" and who is "out." For others, it's far more important to speak of a journey toward the center. John Ortberg states, "In Australia there are two main methods for keeping cattle on the ranch. One is to build a fence around the perimeter. The other is to dig a well in the center of the property. I think Jesus is more like a well than a fence."[26] For still others, the whole conversation is a fallacy;

pitching "in and out" and "far and near" against one another is a category mistake.[27]

Figure 6.1 outlines the four typical sets. It should be clear from the three previous chapters that we're advocating what this figure regards as a well-formed, centered set.

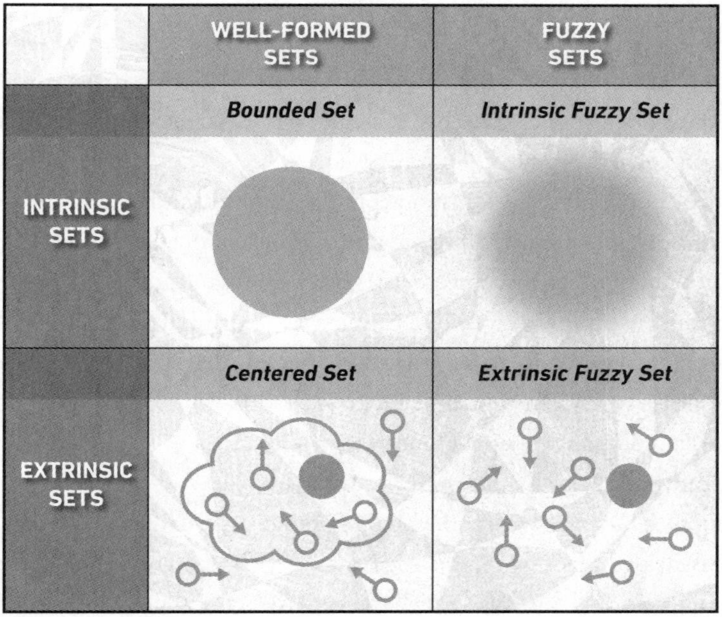

Figure 6.1. Typology of sets[28]

Local churches relate to other churches in different ways and to different ends. We belong to different sets for different reasons. To translate the categories into our discussion so far, a traditional bounded set would be one with a narrow core alone. This is the kind of set that enables level-one and level-two partnerships. For many of us, our denominational affiliations operate in this way. Whatever journey we may be on, we either subscribe to a certain set of theological propositions or we don't; we are either "in" or "out."

At the other end of the spectrum, an intrinsic (or boundaryless) fuzzy set may be defined by a cause alone. There are times when such partnerships are the most appropriate. For example, occasionally diverse groups, not simply from different Christian theological positions but from different faith groups, may stand in solidarity together because of a particular social or legislative issue.

Between these two poles, somewhere in the middle, is a well-formed centered set, which has an essential core but also exists for the sake of a specific cause. This is a level-three partnership, coalescing around a well-articulated box-C vision.

To simply pit sets against one another is to misunderstand the way different ends require different means. For example, a church sometimes functions like a centered-set grouping. As the gospel is preached on Sunday morning, everyone is welcome to drink from the well. We are right to think of Jesus as the well; after all, he is living water. There are times when a movement functions as though there are no boundaries at all and with a generous openness to all.

But he is also the gate and the way (John 10:7; 14:6). So at times churches function with some kind of boundary, usually when it comes to issues of leadership, decision making, baptism, and the Lord's Supper. So there are also times the essential core must be upheld for the cause to be served well.

The basic shape of a collaborative movement is a well-formed centered set. This is what it means to have all three clauses of the equation working together to produce collaboration. In a bounded-set model, the key question is "Am I in, or am I out?" In a centered-set model, the key question is "Where am I heading?" Both are important questions, but there's a distinct value to belong to something that's continually pushing you up and forward in your faith and that keeps asking for your direction of travel, rather than reassuring you that you have already arrived.

The Code of Collaboration

Figure 6.2 builds on figures 4.1 and 5.5 introduced in the previous chapters. The core creates the boundary, the cause creates the center, but the code creates movement. Once the code is added to the formula, the theological vision of the movement "goes live" in a way that energizes the movement for action.

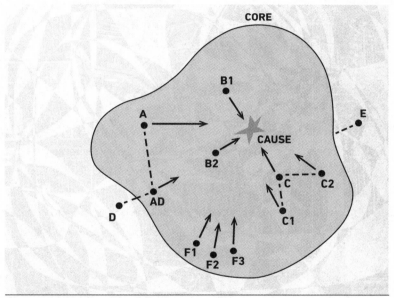

Figure 6.2. The code of collaboration

Through the code, churches that have been "looking in" begin to get excited and energized by the cause, and they decide to partner, churches unconvinced are won over, churches on the fringe are drawn to the center, and churches at the center become leaders by influence.

- Church A has transitioned from simply being a faithful church with informal fellowship with one or two other like-minded churches. It has been won by the DNA code to a greater cause to reach the city for Christ. The result is that Church A has become an active partner in a local collaborative church-planting movement.

- Churches B1, B2, and C, which have already been won to the cause, are now taking active steps to begin to meet the need. They are close to the center and likely to model best practice. As such they are potential influencers of others.

- Church C has already planted two further churches (C1 and C2). Of course, the bonds between these three churches are strong, but because they've been planted with the code of the movement in the DNA of the churches, they're immediately onboard with and contributing to the cause.

- Church D had been outside the core and had lost its way with regards to the gospel. However, as a dying congregation, it reached out to Church A, which has begun a replant of Church D. New leadership, new vision, and a new core of believers has meant a new start for the church, which is now Church AD. It may look like it is on the fringe of the movement, but it is making its way to the center as a work of renewal takes place.

- Churches F1, F2, and F3 had not considered planting to be an option for them, but as they saw what was happening, as the cause was articulated, and as the code got to work, they began actively looking for ways they can play their part in reaching the city.

So figure 6.2 got a little busy, just like real life!

Conclusion

Core plus cause plus code equals collaboration. God willing, all three terms of the equation work together to produce the context for a faithful spiritual movement to flourish. In a sense, it's like the fire triangle. What's needed to make fire? Fuel, oxygen, and heat. Without one of those ingredients, there will be no ignition; but with all three in place, you get fire. Well, when the core, cause, or code is missing, anything you attempt may spark, but it won't become a flame. With all three actively working, you get ignition. You get fire!

Collaboration

No one can whistle a symphony.
It takes a whole orchestra to play it.

HALFORD E. LUCCOCK

In this chapter, you'll learn how collaboration means we can do together what we can't on our own— without losing our own identity. We will explore:

- *the types of collaboration available within a church-planting movement;*
- *the degrees of collaboration available within a church-planting movement; and*
- *the unique beauty of collaboration.*

The Raindrop Theory

Collaborative church-planting movements create a context for level-three partnership in the same way that clouds create the context for precipitation.

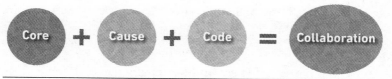

Figure 7.1. The three essentials of collaboration

It may be hard to believe, but scientists are still mystified as to how clouds actually produce rain.[1] But concerning cold-air clouds, one dominant theory has emerged. When warm air rises, it carries tiny water droplets high into the atmosphere, where the temperature is much lower. These microscopic droplets freeze, becoming ice crystals that are just a few microns in size—far too small to fall to the ground. They need to collaborate. The turbulence within the clouds energizes these crystals so they coalesce, creating larger flakes of snow that grow to a size that means they can fall from the sky. Depending on the temperature, they either remain snowflakes or melt on the way down and become rain.

As churches in Birmingham, it isn't difficult for us to see our city as a thirsty land crying out for the water of life. In some communities, there are wonderful signs of life, with spreading vines bearing fruit for Christ. There are rich and humid pockets, but they're scattered and isolated in an otherwise arid environment. We don't claim to know of every work of the gospel going on in our great city, but we are yet to meet another church that doesn't share our prayer for precipitation.

However, as individual churches quietly and carefully planting and watering in our own little corner of the city, we can feel very much like individual ice crystals, just a few micrometers in diameter, without the weight that leads to rain. We need a way of connecting that would mean we could do more together than we can on our own. But it doesn't happen by accident. In fact, rather than coalesce, we have a strong tendency to repel one another. This is particularly the case when we restrict ourselves entirely to level-one and level-two partnerships. We quickly discover that doctrinal distinctives and ministry practices set us apart from one another and rule out collaboration.

A catalyst is needed to move us from repulsion to coalescence. This is what a common core, cause, and code offers; it creates excitement and momentum in order to form rain. Our prayer at 2020birmingham is that we may, under God, be one such cloud.

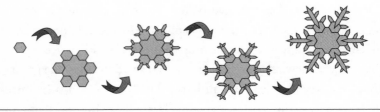

Figure 7.2. Snowflake formation[2]

One of the fears we have about collaboration is that it will result in us losing our own identity, vision, and focus. This is partly why the snowflake analogy is helpful. As ice crystals join, they don't simply form an amalgamated blob. They retain their original shape; but by joining together, they grow big enough to begin to fall. Figure 7.2 shows how this happens. Snowflakes form without distorting the original crystals, and together they create movement.

Now that the three components for collaboration are in place—core, cause, and code—we'll briefly outline the different types and degrees of collaboration that may be employed by a movement in order for churches to retain their identity while becoming part of a bigger vision.

The Difference Between Partnership and Collaboration

Strictly speaking, *partnership* is what happens when distinct parties *work together*. However, *collaboration* goes further and could be defined as what happens when distinct parties *work together to produce something they simply could not produce on their own.* Many times in this book, we've used each word, but they aren't necessarily interchangeable. Partnerships exist for all kinds of reasons. They are real and they are important. But fruitful *partnerships* around a common core, code, and cause are rightly termed *collaborations* because they produce something together that wouldn't have happened otherwise.

For example, Neil and I (John) are partners in the gospel (Philippians 1:5), and that partnership led to the collaborative action of writing a book together. When it comes to 2020birmingham, it's fair to say that there are many churches outside the movement that are true partners in the gospel but that, for whatever reason, haven't chosen to take the step of collaboration yet. One reason is because unless you see yourself as a church-planting church and are planning to plant in the next five years, it's hard to see what kind of a contribution you can make.

This is why it's helpful to speak of *types* and *degrees* of collaboration. If any church embraces all three terms of the formula, there should be a way for them to collaborate. And there is a place for all at the table. No one need feel excluded. Because of the variables involved, you may call this the goldilocks principle. In astronomy, the goldilocks zone is the place in our solar system that our planet occupies because it's neither too hot nor too cold to support life. It's the goldilocks zone because it's *just right* for life to thrive.

Because of the different types and degrees of partnership available in a collaborative movement, whatever the situation a church may be in, it can find its goldilocks zone: the place that is *just right* for it to flourish in advance of the cause.

Types of Collaboration

There are four basic types of collaboration within a church-planting movement: sowing, sending, supplying, and supporting.

1. Sowing. At the center of the movement will be some who are actively involved in planting new churches. This will be by a variety of models and in relationship with their own particular sending churches, networks, and denominations. This is the frontline of the movement as leaders are called by God and their churches, and as they identify priority areas of the city, gather core teams, access training, recruit support, cast vision, create infrastructure, and sow new church plants.

Belonging to the movement means peer-to-peer support with others who are also faithfully stepping out onto the frontline. It means gaining and sharing experiences of the context of the city. It means accessing training that is city-specific and designed to equip those who are in the sowing phase. It means having the opportunity for a mentor who understands in part what the phases of church planting are like. It means having a context where it may be possible to cultivate partnerships with other local churches that may be willing to send, supply, and support.

For example, within 2020birmingham are church planters who have undertaken pioneer church plants or mother-daughter plants, have expanded their church across multiple sites, or have undertaken works of church revitalization. Many of them actively participate in the monthly planters forum; many are receiving training through Incubator, a course to aid church planters in the first couple of years of their plant; and many are involved in some kind of mentoring or coaching relationship.

For John Walley, a "sower" who recently planted a church with 2020birmingham, there was a simple logic to making 2020birmingham his home. He reflects,

> It's fair to say that without 2020birmingham, Christ Church wouldn't exist. First, 2020 gave a vision for our city; it helped us to see how we could plant a church in a partnership with existing

churches, with others around us to support and help us planters. Second, 2020 was a banner that helped us gather others to the work we were doing. Our church plant became a bigger project than just a plan that we had in our small church. It became something that other churches wanted to hear about, pray for, and support. People joining the core team had already heard of 2020 and so were more easily able to commit as they were part of something bigger. Lastly, 2020 has been an ongoing source of friendship, training, and support. I was attending 2020 meetups for two years before we planted, which was a source of huge encouragement, wisdom, and blessing as I planned to plant. That support has only grown and continued since we've planted.

2. Sending. Around those who are actively sowing are the churches that are sending and supporting them. These may be individuals but may also be church communities and mission agencies with a commitment to church planting embedded in their DNA, actively working to see churches planted. They may be relatively new or long established; either way they're seeking to create new pioneering opportunities for the gospel. They may be actively raising up leaders to be the next generation of church planters. They may be actively setting aside the resources that will allow them to move quickly when the time is right. They may be contributing to the conversation identifying the spiritual need across the city.

Belonging to the movement means knowing that whoever is sent will be supported, not just by the sending church but also by a band of practitioners who care deeply that the plant will succeed. It means being able to talk at an early stage about where, when, and how a church plant may take place in a way that will allow it to meet the spiritual need of the city and enable it to flourish quickly. It means not having to send people in isolation but with the option of partnerships with other churches, which may mean things progress more quickly and become viable earlier.

For example, the three leaders that laid the foundations for 2020birmingham were not at the time planning to lead new church plants themselves; they were leading churches that were raising up leaders and core teams, preparing to send out others to plant in the city. It was, in part, a concern for the health and long-term viability of these new church plants that led them to gather around the table and talk.

When I (John) began to discuss the revitalization project that became the first 2020birmingham church plant, a number of local sending churches played a part in it coming to fruition. I was trained and sent by City Church (the church Neil pastors). They also joined with two other sending churches to provide a core team of people to help with the work. Beyond that, as we began, a number of other churches sent financial support to enable us to get things off the ground. At the time, none of those churches claimed the revitalization as their own project; the church that had invited us in took ownership of its own revitalization. Around it was a whole network of senders enabling it to happen.

3. Supplying. Around those who are sowing and sending are the churches, parachurch organizations, and individuals that have a role to play in supplying an active contribution when a new initiative is launched. This may be in the form of commissioning some core team members to something that isn't their own initiative but that they're excited to see happening. It may be a hands-on partnership looking to supply from the sidelines something the plant lacks. It may be supplying administrative support, an occasional team of volunteers, helpful local knowledge, or mentoring. They themselves do not have a hand in forming or directing the vision of the plant, but they recognize they have something to offer that may just meet a need.

Belonging to the movement means having the confidence to supply people for a project that's well-conceived and well-supported. It means having a forum to gain knowledge of the kinds of needs in which they may be able to play a part. It means growing in generosity as the box-C vision takes hold and there's an urgent desire to give away something to the cause.

Kenny, one of our American partners, brings a very helpful perspective on this type of collaboration. He is a strategy leader for the International Mission Board church-planting team for the United Kingdom outside London. He has been with 2020birmingham from the very beginning and has partnered with a British church planter named Jez, who has planted a church in north Birmingham. He describes his role this way: "I am a bit of a shadow pastor, not leading from the front. Jez is clearly a visionary, a lead elder of our church, rightly so. I see my role as just being behind him to hold him up, to encourage him, to pray for him, to be a sounding board for him, but also to be a source of fresh ideas, maybe looking at things from different angles."

It's particularly interesting to see how the relationship between 2020birmingham and the International Mission Board has developed through Kenny. He wrote,

> When we started, I was the only American. From the beginning I could see where we as a mission sending agency could potentially come into 2020birmingham and have a role to be catalytic and resourceful, and to be encouraging and to help co-lead potential church plants across the city. And so that has happened over time. Now we have multiple IMB and other American sending agencies who are part of 2020.

It's exciting to see both Americans and Brits partnering around a common core, cause, and code. Kenny notes, "It's just this wonderful partnership of local British pastors and churches who have a heart to do this. I'm working with American missionaries who have the same heart for the city. When we share a burden, the burden is halved, and so we are sharing the burden with one another, for the sake of the gospel."

The implications of this are very exciting. Kenny recognizes a hugely important shift in strategy that's taking place within IMB and other mission agencies:

The approach to church planting on the field used to be to send an American missionary family to a place of service and for them to start just left of zero. I mean start with no partners, no connections, no relationships, and just to crack on with the work of church planting. For those who are really apostolically gifted, that can work out. But it still doesn't mean it's the best way to do it. And so, to be truthful, I think in many cases we almost acted as if the church didn't already exist.

Now we have a change of strategy. We are beginning to say, "It's time that we look at the local church and how we can potentially work together for the purpose of making disciples and church planting." We are beginning to let the local church determine the strategy on the field.

In the long run, this will lead to a more fruitful approach to church planting for everyone, Kenny notes.

We don't want to act as if the local church doesn't already exist. We don't want to work around it. We want to plant local churches that reflect the culture and community in which the church is planted. And here's the thing as cultural outsiders: How do we know how to do that? Well, the truth is, we don't. We can read all the books about England. We can watch *Downton Abbey*, but that doesn't make us English.

To plant a church that is going to reach out to working-class families it becomes vital to work with national partners so we can plant churches that reflect their culture. That's the end goal: to assist in the planting of churches which reflect the community and culture in which they're planted. This also has added stability. If the missionary gets sent home or their visa is denied, the work won't collapse.

I think this is the way forward. We're seeing it work in 2020birmingham. We're seeing people come to the Lord in ones and twos; we're seeing disciples made; and we're seeing local churches strengthened and planted.

4. Supporting. Around these three types of collaboration are churches, parachurch organizations, and individuals committed to supporting church plants but aren't in a place to do their own planting. But they love the fact that planting is going on in their city, and they're keen to support the work. They may be willing to contribute something financially; they may be actively praying for each new plant; they may collaborate by visiting, volunteering with, praying for, and giving to or even adopting a particular plant.

Belonging to the movement means being resourced with knowledge about what's going on in the city so you can pray, give, and visit, confident that you're supporting something that's serving this bigger vision. Belonging to the movement means you aren't just hearing about something that other churches are doing, and you aren't just on the sidelines looking in. You are a part of what God is doing through the churches in the city.

Around 2020birmingham are some remarkable supporters. Over the years we've run a number of fundraising dinners and gathered a number of people who love the core, love the cause, and love the code of what we're seeking to do. People have given generously at crucial moments to help us fund infrastructure and projects that are needed. They're quietly and faithfully championing what's happening and contributing sacrificially to enable things to happen.

Organizations are supportive too. Briarwood Presbyterian Church in Birmingham, Alabama, has committed to long-term prayer and financial support. They have given money to two of our seventeen projects and are looking forward to further collaboration over the longer term. It's exciting to have built a "Birmingham to Birmingham" partnership, even though our cities look so different on the ground. What a joy to know there are Christians on the other side of the Atlantic cheering us on with every step we take!

We're also developing a whole lattice of prayer support around the world. We publish a printed prayer guide twice a year. It's also possible to receive a daily prayer request for a 2020birmingham church plant via a prayer app. We have subscribers in a number of different countries around the world as people share the vision and want to support what's happening.

A couple of years ago Andy Weatherley and I (John) had the privilege of being invited to the mission conference of a large church in Seoul with a heart for church planting and revitalization across Europe. It was humbling to witness tens of thousands of Christians praying in Korean for our dear city of Birmingham. We know they continue to pray. This type of collaboration may be geographically distant, but it's no less important.

Degrees of Collaboration

There's not only a variety of types of collaboration but also degrees of collaboration. Remember the goldilocks zone? It's possible to find the right zone, neither too hot nor too cold, for you to flourish in the movement and play your part. One good way to understand the degrees of collaboration available is to illustrate them as four concentric rings, illustrated by figure 7.3.

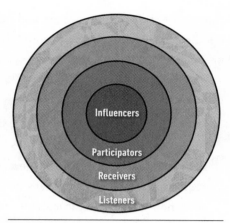

1. Listeners. Moving from the outer circle in, this is first degree of collaboration. Some individuals and church representatives position themselves on the edge of the movement, almost eavesdropping. Col-

Figure 7.3. Degrees of collaboration

laboration requires trust, and it can take time to establish whether a movement is something worth belonging to or not. It's possible simply to turn up and listen in to most of our gatherings; in fact, it's actively encouraged.

For 2020birmingham, there are a number of folk we will see only a few times a year, perhaps at a conference or a workshop, who are attempting to discern at their own pace if this movement is for them. It may be tempting to disregard this outer circle as beyond the parameters of collaboration, but we want to recognize that these people are very welcome, and we trust that it's beneficial for them to connect in this way. We don't place expectations on them. If a movement is to remain organic and spontaneous, we must be open to the DNA code being caught and multiplied without any further relationship with the movement center and regardless of whether churches become participating players in a recognizable way. However, listening is often the gateway for them to move inward toward deeper levels of involvement.

We could name a number of people who are currently listening in to what we're doing, attending the planters forum, having significant conversations behind the scenes, and figuring out what it may mean for them to move toward a deeper level of involvement. It isn't appropriate to tell their stories at this point. However, many participants and influencers within 2020birmingham first started to engage by listening in to what was happening.

Hilary, who is church planting with her husband, Stu, writes,

> I value how 2020birmingham is a community where we can share ideas with other church planters, pray for one another, and hear stories that remind us that God is bringing the hope of the good news to people throughout our city. I enjoy and benefit from the training times and appreciate being reminded of the bigger picture of how God is at work. I am so grateful for 2020birmingham and the chance to encourage and learn from one another.

Hilary and Stu may have begun by listening, but they quickly realized how valuable this context is, and they are now among a group of key participators.

2. Receivers. In one sense, listening is a passive form of receiving, but for receivers there's a desire to connect relationally with others within the movement because of a conviction that this is something to join. 2020birmingham continues to offer more ways to receive input, such as

- the planters forum, a monthly gathering for prayer, support, and encouragement for planters;

- Incubator, a two-year-long, one-day-a-month training course for planters;

- Next Generation evenings, where keen members and future leaders gather to gain insight into the vision and values of 2020birmingham; and

- connecting with another church within the movement through a mentoring relationship.

Again, there is no expectation that any individual or church must pay the group back. There are some who belong to 2020birmingham for whom giving is not an option. There are some for whom the movement was a stage in the development of their plant, but there is little in the way of an ongoing relationship. It's key to the principle of generosity that those who wish simply to receive are welcome to come and do so. If this serves the kingdom of God, it is to be celebrated. Abraham writes,

> I am a planter and one of the leaders of the Ethiopian Evangelical Church in Birmingham. At the early stage of our church plant, I learned about 2020birmingham through City Church, where my family and I were members. As a planter, I was so much in need of a company of fellow planters. We earnestly prayed for each other's needs, studied various biblical and theological topics, and shared testimonies of God's help. These were times of great blessing and a source of great encouragement to me. 2020birmingham facilitated the finding of a meeting place for our church in an area where most of our members lived. Also, the various conferences and seminars have blessed me personally. Being part of 2020birmingham allowed us to participate in God's bigger work in Birmingham, in the advancing of his kingdom among all people and ethnic minorities in our city.

Right now, Abraham is a church-planting catalyst among Ethiopians in the United Kingdom. However, without a doubt, it played a small but important part in helping him plant this first Ethiopian church. The relationship with Abraham and the church continues, and 2020birmingham may have a role to play again in the future.

3. Participators. Many who first simply come to receive begin to see how they may play an active part. Participation isn't dictated from above; it's something that people begin to work out for themselves as they see a need and want to meet it. Key to the health of the movement is a growing body of knowledge. As movement members increase in experience, they have wisdom to share.

At our monthly planters forums, participation is actively encouraged as we discuss evangelism, discipleship, church organization, crosscultural mission, contextualization, growing multiethnic churches, estate ministry, and so on. No one individual is an expert, but the greater the participation, the richer the shared knowledge. Participation is about adding value to aspects of the movement as you imbibe the code and begin to make a contribution.

Parakaleo is a group established to support the spouses of church planters, which in our context means planters' wives. Jo Weatherley explains the need and the vision for it:

> As I reflected on my experience as a church planter's wife and talked with other women involved in church planting, I was really burdened for the spiritual and emotional well-being of the wives of planters. It's such an ambiguous role, with wives often juggling supporting the planter, extra responsibilities at the church plant, family responsibilities, and employment outside church. Yet they have often not had formal theological training and are unable to take part in many of the supportive elements of 2020.
>
> The vision of Parakaleo is still evolving, but we meet together regularly to sharpen each other in the gospel, learn from each other's experiences, and discuss key heart issues that affect our passion for Jesus and his church as we serve. For example, last time we met, we looked at our own need of the gospel and

the extent to which we minister by grace. I would hope that as we meet together, this group is a safe place to be open about the challenges we face (but not a pity party!) and that relationships will flow out of that which can be precious over many years of ministry.

Ro is one of group's participants. She is married to Barnaby, and they are about a year into their church revitalization project. She reflects,

> The most helpful aspect of Parakaleo so far is the understanding and encouragement from ladies further down the road. They've been through our stage in terms of church and family life, so they can hold out hope and wisdom from their experiences. We're still getting to know each other, but I trust that with time this will be a really safe space to study, share, eat cake, cry, laugh, and pray together. It already encouraged me to reach out to a couple of wives from the groups when I needed a chat with someone outside church but with inside knowledge of the challenges we face.

Parakaleo highlights just how important collaboration is. We really do need each other, and the active participation of people from different cultures and generations only makes things stronger. Jo wrote,

> It is great to have women from different seasons of life together, ranging from those who have years of experience planting cross-culturally and who have raised children while serving in ministry to those in their first year of planting with preschool children. It's particularly encouraging to have those who have walked the path before, who have wisdom to share.

This particular context for collaborative participation is full of the 2020birmingham DNA code. Hilary said, "Parakaleo gives us a chance to remind one another that no matter how family or work responsibilities influence our diaries, we are part of a movement of God bigger than ourselves."

4. Influencers. Once people are participating in a movement, it doesn't take long before they identify areas in which it can be improved, strengthened, and resourced in ways that serve the cause. At this point, a partner moves from simply participating to actively influencing the development and direction of the movement. This involves building on a foundation that has already been laid or extending what the movement can do.

There should be room in a collaborative movement for listeners to become receivers, for receivers to become participators, and for participators to become influencers so that the movement can continue to multiply.

Of course Jonathan, Neil, and Andy are key influences within 2020birmingham. However, many others quoted throughout this book have moved from the edge to the center, taking responsibility for particular aspects of the fledgling movement and helping it grow. People also are growing in influence in their particular areas of ministry. They're training others in discipleship, evangelism, church revitalization, and crosscultural mission. They're telling their stories to inspire and help others. Some are simply stepping up and serving behind the scenes.

One of our prayers is that as more people make their way to the center of 2020birmingham, there will be an increasing level of diversity among the influencers. It has been important to give people who clearly have expertise in certain areas permission to lead.

We're always grappling with what it will mean for us to grow into a movement that truly impacts the city as a whole, not only with church planting but also with other specializations—such as justice and mercy ministries, and faith and work initiatives—that would create something of a gospel ecosystem. This will mean inviting others serving within the city to join and to exercise influence within the group.

Conclusion

If you take a tray of ice cubes out of a freezer, you see that each is a homogenous block of frozen water—no character, no difference, just pure utility. Contrast that with a snowflake. The collaborative effect of myriad frozen particles creates phenomenal and nimble beauty—and no two flakes are alike. The miracle of snowfall caused American philosopher Henry David Thoreau to remark, "How full of the creative genius is the air in which these are generated! I should hardly admire more if real stars fell and lodged on my coat. Nature is full of genius, full of the divinity; so that not a snowflake escapes its fashioning hand."[3]

The types and degrees of collaboration that make up a movement give it its unique shape and identity. The distinctive of each constituent member is preserved, yet the whole is somehow great than the sum of the parts. Only through a joining can snow happen, and there remains something miraculous about that joining. We must be careful not to reduce God's sovereign work of church planting to a mere formula.

When ice crystals coalesce, they retain their original shape while growing together and belonging to something bigger. This allows each crystal to preserve its own identity. But it also means that each resulting snowflake is unique. It really is true that no two flakes are the same. And this is just as true for collaborative church-planting movements. Movement "science" means that no two city initiatives will be the same.

We've been approaching the formation of collaborative church-planting movements from three different yet complementary and interdependent perspectives.[4] Part one of the book outlined the *norm*, identifying a biblically mandated commission that demands a box-C vision. Part two outlined the *context*, showing how time and place cultivate a shared theological vision that allows for level-three partnerships. Part three will now focus on the *person*. It will seek to show how you and the relationships you develop bring an important and unique contribution to the whole. We could call this the X Factor.

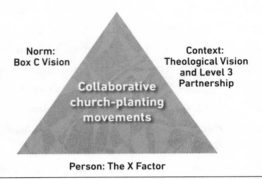

Figure 7.4. Norm, context, and person

Figure 7.4 shows how this works. Let's explore two brief reflections. First, all three perspectives are required to understand how collaborative church-planting movements are possible. These perspectives are three sides of the triangle. They don't compete against each other; they work together to bring about something that is faithful to Scripture and yet utterly suited to the person God has made you to be and the context he has placed you in.

Second, although we've become more used to talking about the importance of context, we often overlook the personal. We compare ourselves with others, see a common theology and a common context, and still wonder how what we're doing is so different. This could become a source of frustration and disillusionment if we lose sight of the personal perspective.

At this point, you may feel envisioned and excited by the possibilities, but you also may be wondering how on earth you can begin along this road and where your partnerships may come from. Well, from our personal perspectives, we can confidently say it won't look the same as 2020birmingham, and that will be a very good thing. It will be a very different snowflake.

It's exciting to think what the X factor means for you. As you read part three, be aware of this. You may not have a Neil Powell or a Jonathan Bell you can partner with, but God has providentially placed you alongside coworkers in God's service, and your field is far too big to farm without collaboration.

PART 3

Who

Taking Part

A man with God on his side is
always in the majority.

JOHN KNOX

This chapter will cover:

- the life cycle of a movement, from the moment we first see the need to the question of completion;
- the life of Nehemiah and the extraordinary faith he exercised at a decisive moment in the history of God's people;
- the life lessons we've been learning as one fledgling city movement; and
- the life questions you may need to answer as you respond to the need before you.

We want to encourage you to consider how you may play your part. We suspect that if you're anything like us, you feel overwhelmed by a task that seems unachievable. But let's remember that we believe in a God who is an expert in the overwhelming and the unachievable.

The Miracle of Dunkirk

After the extraordinary rescue of Dunkirk, Sunday June 9, 1940, was declared a national day of thanksgiving. But how would the nation make sense of what had happened? Churchill described it as a miracle of deliverance—and it was a crucial and timely miracle. The battle of France was over, but the battle of Britain was about to begin. Churchill famously declared, "*Upon this battle depends the survival of Christian civilization. . . . Let us therefore brace ourselves to our duties, and so bear ourselves, that if the British Empire and its Commonwealth last for a thousand years, men will still say, This was their finest hour.*"[1]

But where had this resolve come from? Where had it begun? One month earlier, days before Dunkirk, on the evening of the May 8, Churchill had addressed the House of Commons with these words: "Let pre-war feuds die; let personal quarrels be forgotten, and let us keep our hatreds for the common enemy. Let party interest be ignored, let all our energies be harnessed, let the whole ability and forces of the nation be hurled into the struggle, and let all the strong horses be pulling on the collar."[2]

This vision for collaborative action was one of the catalysts for the resignation of Neville Chamberlain as prime minister, his replacement by Churchill, the formation of a national coalition government that united parliamentarians across party boundaries, and the beginning of a united fight against the enemy. The need was urgent and over-whelming. A timely coalition around a common cause set in motion the most unlikely series of events and the most extraordinary victory.

From a human perspective, with Churchill we may say, "Upon this battle depends the survival of Christianity." Who will hurl themselves into the struggle? We must respond to the desperate need of our communities. And, in light of the vast opportunity, as Christians living under the reign of the risen and ascended Lord Jesus Christ, unlikely events and extraordinary victories ought to be our common currency! May "pre-war feuds" and "personal quarrels" be forgotten as we strive together toward a bigger vision and see a true miracle of deliverance.

But where do we begin?

Nehemiah's Kingdom Concern

As you consider the part you'll play in this bigger vision, reflect for a moment on another miracle of deliverance in another time and place among God's people.

It is 446 BC, a real low point for Israel. They had been exiled under Assyria and further dismantled as a nation under Babylon. Now under Persian rule, some have returned to the land, but they are weak, vulnerable, and lacking in faith and vision. Nehemiah is comfortable in exile, as one of the Persian king's assistants, but Jerusalem lies in ruins. It's time for unlikely events and extraordinary victories.

Prayer and providence. Word comes to Nehemiah that "those who survived the exile and are back in the province are in great trouble and disgrace. The wall of Jerusalem is broken down, and its gates have been burned with fire" (Nehemiah 1:3). No walls means no royal city, which means no nation.

What will Nehemiah do? Send them a card? Form a committee? Set up a crowdfunding page? "When I heard these things, I sat down and wept. For some days I mourned and fasted and prayed before the God of heaven" (1:4). A kingdom in ruins leaves a man in ruins. And yet this may be Nehemiah's finest hour. Movement leader Terry Virgo says, "Until we have wept over the ruins we will never build the wall."[3] Building begins with brokenness.

Nehemiah begins to pray. God is God, and Nehemiah is not. He comes with empty hands and reminds God of his own promise to gather back the exiles, saying, "They are your servants and your people, whom you redeemed by your great strength and your mighty hand" (Nehemiah 1:10). God is not asked to sanctify Nehemiah's puny plans, but to fulfill his promises and finish what he started.

So, will you pray? Prayer is essential—and easily neglected. We gladly gather to strategize, but do we gather as part of our worship of God? A large portion of 2020birmingham's monthly planters forum is given over to sharing, giving thanks, praising, and petitioning God together. We're learning to pray more fervently, more accurately, more compassionately, and more expectantly as we bring our different cultural practices together.

Recently we've realized as a group that we haven't prayed enough for Birmingham. God, in his grace, has given us growth despite our prayerlessness. We've made it our goal to recruit one hundred global prayer partners within the next year, who will pray daily for the city and the church plants within 2020birmingham. Our goal is to have one thousand prayer partners within the next five years. What might God do if we earnestly seek him? As the apostle James wrote, "You do not have because you do not ask God" (James 4:2).

Finally, Nehemiah prayed, "Give your servant success today by granting him favor in the presence of this man" (Nehemiah 1:11). Which man? He says, "I was cupbearer to the king." In the providence of God, Nehemiah had access to none other than the king of Persia.

Please don't think that movements are all about methodology. God alone gives the growth, and in his providence, sometimes the best-laid plans do not come to pass. Two groups of churches in different cities may begin a movement in the same way, and yet in five years they will look completely different and experience different degrees of momentum and achievement. We must not get into the comparison game. God has a role for us to play in the context he has put us in. Trust him; he knows what he's doing.

Our response to the challenges of our communities begins with prayer and providence. Jesus said, "On this rock, I will build my church, and the gates of Hades will not overcome it" (Matthew 16:18). He promised to finish what he started. Will we humble ourselves and cry out to him? And will we open our eyes and discover that he also has us just where he wants us?

Risk and the Miraculous

What happened next is both reassuring and challenging. Nehemiah said, "I was very much afraid" (Nehemiah 2:2). He had to speak to the king, but he was filled with fear. He was just like us! Now, if it were me, this would read, "I was very much afraid, so I kept my mouth shut." But it doesn't. It reads, "I was very much afraid, but I said to the king . . . 'The city where my ancestors are buried lies in ruins, and its gates have been destroyed by fire'" (2:2-3). Fear is a prelude to courage.

The king asked Nehemiah what he wanted, and we are told, "Then I prayed to the God of heaven, and answered the king" (2:4-5). This was Nehemiah's moment for action, and with a quick prayer, he took the risk and spoke boldly: "Send me to the city . . . so I that can rebuild it" (2:5). Overwhelmed by the need and provided with an opportunity, Nehemiah put his life on the line for the kingdom of God.

You are not the cause of growth, but you do influence growth. Only God can bring about a spiritual movement, but he invites us to take prayerful, courageous risks for him. Here is the paradox: a local collaborative church-planting movement comes down to the sovereign work of God, but it won't happen if you don't act. As you trust God, do something. Pray like it all depends on God, and work like it all depends on you.

Nehemiah was a catalyst. He turned the vision into reality and got things going. As far as we know, he was not a charismatic figure, but he led Israel into action at the crucial moment—and it all began there. Catalytic leaders, who are creative, imaginative, bold, visionary, and zealous, are a primary component for a transdenominational movement of the gospel to flourish in a city.

Business writer Jim Collins said, "The good-to-great leaders never wanted to become larger-than-life heroes. They never aspired to be put on a pedestal or become unreachable icons. They were seemingly ordinary people quietly producing extraordinary results."[4] In their book *Churches Partnering Together*, Chris Bruno and Matt Dirks ask, "Has God provided the right catalytic leader for a new partnership? Or is the potential leader just someone who's excited about this ministry (there's a big difference)? Is he a proven shepherd-hearted, entrepreneurial leader who can rally others around a new project?"[5]

Within 2020birmingham, we've found that having two catalytic leaders from different tribes is remarkably helpful. Jonathan and Neil were experienced church planters in the city, and their churches had already gone on to plant daughter churches. They were known, respected, and trusted by fellow city leaders. They write,

> We're not sure you birth a city movement through a big committee, but equally, it's probably not something best attempted on your own. In our experience, busy pastors are often quite good at starting new ideas but not so good at seeing them through. In our own city, we've seen some very good initiatives come and go. But our commitment to a bigger vision and a ten-year plan was

cemented by our commitment to one another. From the outset, we shared a strong sense of ownership. By leading together, we were able to inspire each other; by leading just the two of us, we were able to keep things focused. The model has helped us get going and keep momentum.

Are you praying for God to provide catalytic leaders who will get things going?

Or are you an answer to that prayer? If so, take courage and get going.

For Nehemiah, the impossible then happened. "It pleased the king to send me" (Nehemiah 2:6). He was also given letters from the king that gave him access to everything he needed to get the job done. Don't miss the miracle here. King Artaxerxes ordered the earlier exiles to stop building anything (Ezra 4:21). Now Nehemiah was returning to the land with a royal consort, signaling a Persian policy U-turn. We all know how governments hate U-turns.

The miracle isn't lost on Nehemiah. He had been tenacious, smart, and brave, but he knew it wasn't down to him. "Because the gracious hand of my God was on me, the king granted my requests" (Nehemiah 2:8). Against all odds, we must take courageous risks, and God will build his kingdom.

Conception

Nehemiah arrived in Jerusalem and inspected the walls. God had put a tremendous vision in his heart; but before he went public, he took a tour of the walls to get the lay of the land, recalling, "I set out during the night with a few others" (Nehemiah 2:12). This was a secret midnight mission with a select few and before anything was announced. Only afterward did he share the vision more widely. He returned to the city after his tour of the walls and said to the Jewish leaders, "You see the trouble we are in: Jerusalem lies in ruins, and its gates have been burned with fire. Come, let us rebuild the wall of Jerusalem, and we will no longer be in disgrace" (2:17).

Don't be in a hurry to go big. I (Neil) have sat in discussions with city leaders trying to figure out the best way to begin, and we found that there can be a strong desire to create a large launch event, gathering widely, with a clear plan of action already in place. However, it may be far more helpful to start small with the right DNA code in place before you seek organic growth.

For 2020birmingham, the "who" question came before the "what" question. Get the right people with the right vision on the bus, and you'll start to know what to do. Look for those who understand the equation for collaboration. Do they love the Lord Jesus—that is, do they share the core? Do they love the city—that is, do they share the cause? Are they committed to church planting and collaboration— that is, do they share the code?

In practice, that may mean drinking quite a few cups of coffee with leaders over six to twelve months before you have the confidence to get going, but those foundational relationships will be key to whatever follows. If the values of fidelity, urgency, compassion, generosity, and humility are in place with just a few of you, it will preserve the culture as you grow.

Go for relational strength. You can't force collaboration, and you shouldn't try. Instead focus on creating the right conditions that will— God willing—enable a sustainable, healthy movement dynamic to develop. We wouldn't advise making it your first ambition to unite or transform the city. Pray that others would join you, but begin with an organic, bottom-up movement of planters committed as much to one another as to the cause. You will know when you have something worth going public with.

SPIRIT, STRATEGY, AND STRUCTURE ANALYSIS

A spirit, strategy, and structure analysis may be a helpful tool to discern if you have a meaningful partnership around the gospel.

Spirit. Do you have enough people around the table who share a common spirit? Do you share the same values? Is there a desire for kingdom collaboration? Is there mutual respect? Has that been evidenced in meetings so far? Do you listen well to one another, defer to one another, prefer one another's interests? Are you committed to working for the greater good? Are you ready to count the cost?

Strategy. Is this a group of leaders united by a common and compelling vision of the future? Can you paint a picture of what you're looking to achieve, and can you see how you may get there? Bruno and Dirks suggest the following diagnostic questions to assess whether there is a clear enough goal:

- Is there an obvious need shared by all?
- Is there an opportunity for partnership?
- Is there congruity? Do those involved have the same strength and quality of commitment?[6]

It's crucial that key leaders are excited and energized by the vision. Bruno and Dirks write, "In the early days of any movement, the main actors often work without compensation. . . . The satisfaction of realized goals is their main reward."[7]

Structure. The third component is structure. How will you go about fulfilling the goal? What are the next steps? Who is responsible for what? Do you have the capacity? For how long and to what degree can you commit? Do you have a sense of ownership?

Work out a timetable for initial meetings. Perhaps aim for three or four meetings over an initial year. If possible, involve a facilitator from outside the city with experience in leading this kind of discussion. Develop a list of prospective participants, which may be somewhere between four and ten church planters.

In your first meeting, spend time making introductions and discussing the big idea. Explain why you've gathered. Share your own stories, and hear how collaborative movements have happened elsewhere. Pray together for one another and the city. Ask, "Would you *like* to meet again?" Be intentional about a second meeting. Set a date, time, and venue.

In your second meeting, together take time to explore what forming a fledgling movement may mean. Describe and define what a local collaborative church-planting movement may look like for you. Use this book if it's helpful. You may consider using the model of 2020birmingham or of one mentioned in the next chapter. Try to discern together the level of congruity. You may all agree in principle, but are you willing to commit to the same degree? Identify what God is already doing in the city as well as the clear needs. Encourage each other, pray together, and foster the dynamics you would want others to experience if they were to join you.

In your third meeting, decide together if this is what everyone really wants to do. After attendees have reflected on the vision and spent time together, ask the question "Do we want to form a local collaborative church-planting movement?" If the answer is no, be thankful that you're enjoying a greater degree of fellowship than before, and consider continuing to meet with a lower level of commitment. If the answer is yes, the focus of the meeting will be planning first steps.

Don't be discouraged if people say no. Jon Dennis of the Chicago Partnership for Church Planting makes a helpful observation based on his experience in Chicago. A new initiative like a church-planting movement may need to start with a younger generation of leaders. He comments, "Don't be surprised if the older generation of leaders say no to an invitation. They may simply have too much invested in other relationships and opportunities to take this on." The lead pastor may not have the capacity to take on another project, but a second pastor or associate pastor may be the key contact to connect with about the idea.

Collaboration

Now, if we were writing the Bible (a dangerous way to begin a statement!), we'd cut out chapter three of Nehemiah altogether, because it seems so boring. It's a long list of people, at least forty-one different teams, and the sections of the wall they rebuilt. For example, we learn that "the Fish Gate was rebuilt by the sons of Hassenaah. They laid its beams and put its doors and bolts and bars in place" (Nehemiah 3:3). So what? Spare us the details!

But that is the whole point. Chapter three is a beautiful study in types and degrees of collaboration. Some get gates, some get walls, some get towers. Some are part of a team, some work on their own, some work as a family enterprise. There are different professions, skill sets, and gifts. Some are local rulers; others are very ordinary. Some are given small tasks; others achieve an incredible amount. Meremoth, son of Uriah, son of Hakkoz, is like a construction machine, appearing twice in the list, while Nehemiah himself, the apparent hero of the tale, isn't mentioned at all. This is a very healthy thing.

Movements, like all living things, follow a recognizable and predictable pattern of birth, growth, maturity, and decline. So learn how to act your age, and stay healthy. You may start well with an initiative

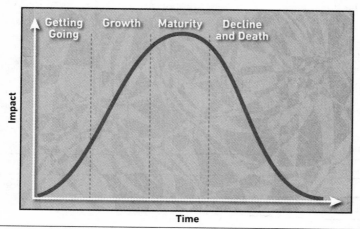

Figure 8.1. Bell-shaped growth curve for movements

for your city, but can you put in place all that's needed to facilitate a self-sustaining movement of the gospel? Figure 8.1 reflects the well-documented dynamics of any living organism.

2020birmingham is slowly progressing through this graph. Our vision and values are unchanged, but as things have grown, we have needed to build for growth. After the first couple of years, I (Neil) realized I couldn't continue to lead 2020birmingham while also managing all of my responsibilities as a pastor. The solution was for an outside donor to fund my administration time. It wasn't a large sum of money, but it enabled me to receive ten hours of administrative support each week. In the past year, we've raised enough money to set aside Andy, one of our most experienced planters, to begin to work as a trainer within 2020birmingham. As we increased the vision, we quickly identified that a key priority for us was to establish something of a training pipeline that would provide the infrastructure for God to raise up the next generation of church planters for the city. To do this entirely reliant on the good will and free time of those within the group was unrealistic, and so getting organized has been key.

The bottom line is that, like Nehemiah, you'll need as much help as you can get. In the early years, heavy lifting depends on already-busy church leaders giving time to getting things going. Set realistic, measurable goals for growth and greater collaboration. And keep asking the question, "Who can help us?"

Architects need builders, and so in due course, catalysts need to recruit and assess a team of willing participants to the cause. It's unusual for a catalyst to have the skills, time, or capacity for movement development. Visionary leaders are rarely the ones who implement the vision. Without builders and their systems, everyone gets frustrated quickly.

How will you assess who is right to join? As you begin to grow, potential planters may want to connect with the movement. If you're an open collective, welcoming planters from outside, you need to make a decision on assessment.

Some networks choose to assess each potential planter themselves. However, this is beyond the ability of a small movement starting out. An alternative may be an off-the-shelf assessment tool.[8] 2020birmingham's normal practice is to leave assessments to a planter's primary network and to assess individuals informally when there isn't another option.

Beyond recruitment, where will you find your leaders? Self-sustaining movements raise them up. As we prepare for 2020birmingham's next ten years and a further thirty church plants, we're asking, "What do we need to put in place to raise up a generation of future leaders within our churches?" So we have a program for the curious. Six times a year, for a couple of hours on a weekday evening, we gather young men and women who may be future planters and core-team members, and with them we share the vision and values of 2020birmingham.

RAISING UP CHURCH PLANTERS

The best way to ensure the health of a church-planting movement is to raise up leaders from within. Leaders need to have the following characteristics or to be growing in them:

- **Character.** It's sometimes said that gifting takes you places but only character keeps you there. The greatest threat to the growth of a healthy church is not a lack of finances, resources, or people but the failure of a leader. What evidence can you see that potential partners are people with integrity? Where do you see the fruit of the Spirit and the battle against sin?
- **Convictions.** Do they have a clear grasp of the gospel? Do they embrace a biblical understanding of gospel ministry?

- ▣ **Competence.** Do they have the necessary gifts that go with the church-planting role? Can they faithfully and persuasively preach? Do they have evangelistic gifts? Do they know how to take people with them, to oversee, and to cast vision?
- ▣ **Calling.** Are they and their spouse and other family members sure this is for them?

Will we find our place and play our part in God's mission? We are instruments in his hands, called to work as one for his glory. The book of Nehemiah provides a warning, saying the nobles of Tekoa "would not put their shoulders to the work under their supervisors" (3:5). Literally, "they would not stoop to serve the Lord." They were stiff-necked, perhaps because, as nobles, they felt collaboration was beneath them. They may well have shared the desire to see the city wall rebuilt, but they didn't "get" collaboration. They were on board with the cause but not the code.

When you're looking to achieve a big goal quickly, anyone who shows an interest in planting is a potential answer to prayer. But don't say yes to everyone. Even with a spirit of generosity, you won't be able to work with every planter in the city.

Also don't expect to be an ecumenical movement. 2020birmingham is only as generous as we believe the gospel will allow us to be. The bare-minimum requirement is a commitment to an evangelical orthodoxy. We need to protect the gospel, and just as crucially we need to preserve the DNA of the thing we're seeking to build. Jonathan and Neil have at times functioned as custodians of the vision and values of the movement, ready to say no to planters who wholeheartedly share the cause but who are on a different page when it comes to the core or the code.

Now contrast the nobles of Tekoa with someone named "Malkijah son of Rekab, ruler of the district of Beth Hakkerem" (Nehemiah 3:14). He isn't a well-known hero of Scripture, but he should be. He repaired the Dung Gate, so called because it led to the dump in the Valley of Gehenna, the place Jesus said pictured hell. What a hero, a ruler who rolled up his sleeves, picked up his trowel, and did the worst job on the wall to serve a cause bigger than himself, humble enough to be immortalized as the Dung-Gate Man!

Comradeship

So, is that the end of the story: they worked together and the walls were built? Not quite. What follows was wave after wave of opposition. Mockery, threats, discouragement, and disunity all attempted to disrupt the rebuilding, but God's people stood firm.

What was the secret to success? Above all, they stood because they stood together. Nehemiah advised them, "The work is extensive and spread out, and we are widely separated from each other along the wall. Wherever you hear the sound of the trumpet, join us there. Our God will fight for us!" (4:19-20). Imagine staring into the darkness, alone on the wall, scared witless as the enemy advances, and with a single toot of your horn a huge family of believers appears out of the gloom to surround you, defend you, and encourage you to stand firm. Collaborative comradeship may be just the support you need to endure when the enemy attacks.

Make it your goal to look after one another. Scott Thomas, pastor and US Director for C2C Network, stated succinctly, "Every church leader needs a coach."[9] It's possible to look after structure, strategy, training, and recruitment while overlooking people. If 2020birmingham is truly going to become a self-sustaining movement, we need to know how to grow churches; but it's just as essential to grow planters and their families in the truth of the gospel.

Look after each other by talking about money. For nearly every church planter starting out, generating funds is a time-consuming, difficult, and stressful process. You may not have a large pot of money to hand out, but you can offer advice, and you may be able to introduce planters to potential donors that are keen to support church planting in your city.

Although 2020birmingham doesn't have a lot of money, we've hosted fundraising dinners and made many introductions over the past few years. Increasingly there's a small amount of organic and informal funding happening across the movement as more-established plants commit financially to new, much-needed plants.

Keeping the vision front and center has helped us to stay focused and to track progress. "What number are we at?" is a question we keep asking because of the vision we've set. It's countercultural for British evangelicals to set goals in this way, but it's helpful for raising money. Donors tend to like big vision and increasing numbers.

Get organized. You may need administrative assistance, media support, resource development, or conferences. In the early stages of collaboration, things are intuitive and informal, but when you enter the growth phase, some structure is needed.

Our experience at 2020birmingham is that we're running to keep up, and many people are quietly and sacrificially doing a huge amount behind the scenes. However, God has a wonderful way of giving you what you need just when it's needed. Giving attention to the structure is not an inherently bad thing. Think of a healthy vine. It can get going with little or no structure, but as it grows, a trellis is needed to train its growth.[10] Once a collaborative movement has a vision to plant twenty, thirty, or fifty churches, it needs to get organized.

However, in scaling up for growth, avoid slowing down the movement. Alan Hirsch warned, "To remain truly missional, established organizations need to be very aware of the dangers of institutionalization."[11] Jim Collins referred to this as the bureau-cratic death spiral.[12] Tim Keller wrote, "A strong, dynamic movement, then, occupies this difficult space in the center—the place of tension and balance between being a freewheeling organism and a disci-plined organization."[13] Look after each other, and get organized without killing creativity.

At Completion?

After further struggle, at last comes the news: "The wall was com-pleted on the twenty-fifth of Elul, in fifty-two days. When all our enemies heard about this, all the surrounding nations were afraid and lost their self-confidence, because they realized that this work had been done with the help of our God" (Nehemiah 6:15-16). Renowned theologian and professor J. I. Packer wrote, "When servants of God who find themselves in trouble humbly get on with the job God has given them to do, great grace is regularly given."[14] This is going to have a happy ending!

Nehemiah 12 records a great celebration. After the repopulation of the city and the re-introduction of temple worship, they finally ded-icate the temple. Like them, make sure you take time to celebrate what God is doing. This excites and motivates churches, planters, and po-tential planters alike, and it builds momentum.

However, Nehemiah 12 is not the end. The final chapter of Ne-hemiah is marked by an ongoing compromise among God's people and the ongoing threat of an enemy with a foothold in the city. So the completion feels incomplete.

This is consistent with other aspects of the rebuilding project. When the foundations of the temple were laid, the people gave a great shout of praise, but we're told that "many of the older priests and Levites and family heads, who had seen the former temple, wept aloud when they saw the foundation of this temple being laid" (Ezra 3:12). Maybe they remembered the former temple, under the great kings of history. Maybe they remembered Ezekiel's former vision of a perfect temple that would one day be rebuilt.[15] They looked at the freshly dug foundations, which clearly weren't those of the perfect temple.

What then is the point of such a massive anticlimax? God's people look like they're home, but they aren't home yet. It looks like the end of exile, but it isn't. Ezra through Nehemiah is the middle of the story. And so, those who are waiting for the end are called to live faithfully for God and for a cause that's bigger than themselves in their time and place. This may not be the final hour, but it can still be our finest hour.

So commit to the vision. As demands increase, it's very easy to find reasons to step back from collaboration and to scale back ambitions. But, whatever the challenges and however it looks today, commit to a big vision for the long term.

And commit to one another. It clearly makes a difference when 2020birmingham planters gather that either I (Neil) or Jonathan is there. We set the example by being visibly committed, which matters especially to planters starting out. They know there are others nearby committed to walking with them for the long term.

Maintaining momentum by making changes in creative ways can enable you to move forward. In his book *The Age of Paradox,* Charles Handy takes the bell curve and turns it into a sigmoid curve to describe how and when to implement change to sustain growth.

Part of committing to a bigger vision is committing to change, often at the point where you're enjoying a season of growth. Figure 8.2 makes clear that change needs to happen before decline sets in, when resources, energy, and confidence are high. A new growth curve must begin while the old one can still support it. The new curve grows out of the old.[16] We do this only if we know that we haven't arrived yet, and if, like Nehemiah, we know an end is not really the end.

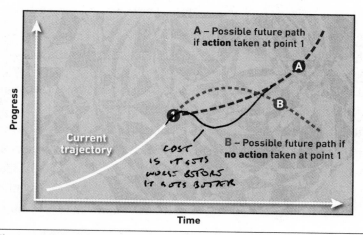

Figure 8.2. Sigmoid-shaped growth curve for movements

Be generous, and make space for new thinkers who can contribute to the further development of the movement. Welcome new initiatives, and be unapologetic in repeating and renewing the vision. What you thought was a big vision may need to get a whole lot bigger. We began by praying for twenty churches, which has become fifty and is growing now into a desire to deeply impact the whole of Birmingham. While planting a church might not be for every church, reaching a city should be. Our prayer is that this vision, shared across strong and weak nodes, the tower and the square, may under God and in the power of the Holy Spirit, really go viral.

At that point you may no longer be a band of brothers and sisters, but you can't afford to become strangers. As you press on, maintain the heart. Prize relationships; they don't stay strong without care. And as you scale up, do so in a way that preserves the priority of relationship. Look for ways you can practically honor and deepen relationships with planters and between churches. And prize the culture of collaboration you've worked so hard to establish. Prize the core, the cause, and the code.

In it all and above all, prize a deep, unashamed, wholehearted dependence on God. Never take growth for granted. The loss of kingdom-focused, other-centered, generous prayer is a sign of a decline long before that decline shows up on a graph. When things go well, pride and self-reliance can quickly follow. Nowhere is that more evident than in a failure to pray.

This side of the death, resurrection, and ascension of Jesus, God has poured out his Spirit, and we are now part of his global restoration project. There is a far greater fulfillment of the promise, but just like Nehemiah, we are also still waiting. We must be wary of a triumphalism, of thinking we've arrived. Local collaborative church-planting movements aren't the final brick in the wall that will usher in the new heavens and the new earth. We must be careful not to speak as though they are. But they are a component of what it means for us, like Nehemiah, to live our lives faithfully for God and for a cause that's bigger than ourselves in our time and place. And, under God, this may become our finest hour. Reflecting on Nehemiah, one author writes,

> There has always been a true elite of God's leaders. . . . They are the meek who inherit the earth (Mt. 5:5). They weep and pray in secret, and defy earth and hell in public. They tremble when faced with danger, but die in their tracks rather than turn back. They are like a shepherd defending his sheep or a mother protecting her young. They sacrifice without grumbling, give without calculating, suffer without groaning. To those in their charge they say, "We live if you do well." Their price is above rubies.[17]

Nehemiah was one of them. What about you?

Together Around the World

In essentials, unity; in non-essentials,
liberty; in all things, charity.

RUPERTUS MELDENIUS

Around the world, God is at work bringing churches together in collaborative partnerships to reach their cities. Each network or movement will inevitably look different from the next; adapted for their own city, they will also reflect the opportunities that arise. In this chapter, we take a tour of the world and interact with five city networks, focusing on a theme of particular importance to that city. As we travel, we learn valuable lessons for our city as we go.

Kingdom Generosity: Evangelio 360 in Valparaiso, Chile

An interview with Patricio Oyarzún, pastor of La Trinidad De Reñaca

Q. Tell us about yourself.

A. (Patricio) I am a Chilean engineer raised to become a businessman who ended up studying theology at Moore College and becoming a church planter of a church supported by City to City. As well I have been involved in setting up a new foundation that is focused on the integration of faith and work in the biotechnological industry. I am married to Dagmar, a gorgeous artist, and we have four young children.

Q. What's unique about your city?

A. We love our city! It is full of life, culture, the sea, and the hills. It is home to one million people; it is the second-biggest city in the country and a UNESCO World Heritage City. Valparaiso is where the Chilean National Congress and the Ministry of Culture are located. Our city's beauty and its prominent role in our country are sadly diminished by the fact that there are very few gospel-centered churches. We need many more!

Q. Tell us a little more about your network.

A. Evangelio 360 (Gospel 360) is made up of a group of pastors and leaders from multiple denominations who pray and work, depending on the power of the Holy Spirit for the changing of our great city of Valparaiso. As we attempt to plant churches that will proclaim the gospel of Christ to the glory of the Father, we work together in raising up the next generation of pastors and leaders.

Q. How did you get started?

A. God placed in the hearts of several pastors and leaders the idea of working together for the sake of the gospel and our city. By God's grace, the movement started as some Presbyterians, Reformed

Anglicans, and independent pastors and leaders met in February 2016, under the inspiration and mentoring of City to City LATAM (Latin America).

Q. **How does a kingdom mindset shape the nature of your movement?**

A. We believe in a generous God who has given us a gospel that compels us to love each other generously. By God's grace, since the very beginning we have been committed to relating to each other in a generous way. This gospel-wrought generosity has been a practical mark of our movement in four main areas: prayer, finances, people, and learning from each other.

When it comes to prayer, we pray in our churches on our main Sunday gatherings for the city network and for specific church plants and their pastors. We believe it is essential that our local churches taste the sweet flavor of partnership that comes out of churches from all around our city and from different denominations working together.

Regarding finances, in 2017 we began the first church plant partially funded by local churches of different denominations. In this case, a Presbyterian church and an Anglican church are helping financially to support a Reformed Methodist Pentecostal church plant.

As well, we have seen several cases of churches encouraging people who have become Christians under their ministry, but who live very far away, to join another church of our city network. We have done so by connecting them with the local pastor or church planter. We believe we work for God's kingdom, not for our own.

Finally, under God, we have developed a generosity-orientated city network culture where we are keen to share the good practices certain local churches have been developing. For example, one church began a great campus work in which they've helped other churches to set up in their local context. Another example is full-time apprentices, people who have already finish their degrees. They leave the workforce for one or two years to serve the church under a qualified pastor so they may explore their potential pastoral calling.

We are so thankful to our God, who has been generous to us in Christ and who has been encouraging us to be generous to each other.

Conclusion. Patricio's story is both humbling and inspiring because it tells of how much can be accomplished when a generous kingdom mindset is at the heart of a movement. It's a beautiful thing when churches are willing to give time, money, people, and prayer for the planting of churches outside their own denomination and tribe. It is also, without doubt, supernaturally inspired. Only God can stir hearts and minds to put aside self-interest in the cause of the kingdom. The challenge is to insist that the movement continues in a spirit of total dependence on God and a culture of persistent prayer in which we continue to ask God to work in and through us for his glory and not our own.

Collaborative Margin: Chicago Partnership for Church Planting in Chicago

An interview with Jon Dennis, pastor of Holy Trinity Church, Chicago

"Our vision is to see a movement of church planting in Chicago that helps Jesus Christ to be tangible in every neighborhood in our city."[1]

Q. Tell us a little about yourself.

A. (Jon) I'm the founding pastor and senior pastor of Holy Trinity Church in Chicago. Married to Amy, we have five children.

Q. How do you persuade established churches in a city to work collaboratively and for the kingdom?

A. Sometimes a small church can do more to start something than a large church. That's what we found here in Chicago.

It has to begin on a platform of mutual trust formed out of relationships that are already there. So, it starts with relationships. We just knew it took time and investment to build trust and understanding. So sometimes it felt slow because you have to have multiple meetings with a group of people.

Second, you need to recognize that trying to bring church cultures together is not very easy. So when we were in the early stages, we had what I call a meeting of the nine, which was three leaders from each of the founding churches. Well, the cultures of church number one and church number two were very different from one another. Church number one was fast—"let's make decisions, let's go now, let's make this happen"—and the other was a historic church that takes a lot of time to make decisions. That meeting erupted. It was not a good meeting. At the meeting of the nine, there were really strong personalities talking over one another, and it was almost like the whole thing came apart at that moment. We had to circle back and pull everyone back together.

So there is a clash of cultures that can happen, and you need long-term persevering leadership that's really patient and willing to keep building those relationships. A maverick personality can get it started, but there's a danger he or she can also turn people off, and then they don't want to partner anymore.

Third, you need a compelling strategy and vision. God sometimes plants a seed of a vision that other people can see when they hear it, and they want to join it. So what we had, that was really needed, was some vision and strategy. Other churches had the broadest level of commitment to doing something in the city, but there was no strategy to it. What came out of our conversations early on was a mutually implanted vision from the Lord. There was a sense of a calling from the Lord that was mutual. But because we had a little bit more of a strategy sketched out, it was like, "We're not gonna reinvent the wheel. Let's go with the strategy that you have kind of laid out."

Q. **How do you persuade busy pastors with lots going on to make this a priority?**

A. You have to look for people that have collaborative margin in their schedule. There are some pastors who know they have zero collaborative margin. They like to collaborate; they just don't have any time in their schedule. But there's a certain personality type or a certain person who has vision for the city who's willing to say, "I'm gonna give a percent of my time to this initiative." They have collaborative margin, and they're willing to make time to have a cup of coffee with a new church planter or someone else.

I actually believe it's spiritual—finding the leaders in the city that have the space for collaborative margin. Those are the ones who are going to build a movement. And oftentimes those will be a number-two leader in a church, not a number-one leader. The number-one leader will be harder driving, and then there will be another leader within the group with capacity. The number-one may sign off on the vision if there's a number-two leader that will implement the vision.

Q. **Any advice on how to talk to potential partners?**

A. Look for leaders that have collaborative margin in their schedule, and don't ask too much of them. Be specific and narrow in how much you ask of them, and then leverage their strengths and their gifts in what they're already doing. So maybe one guy's already good at coaching. Make him the coach. Is this guy great at putting events together? Just ask him to do a very small thing but help to build a team that does the whole thing.

Q. **And your goal as a movement for Chicago?**

A. The vision is to plant one hundred churches together. Right now, we've planted about twenty-one churches together, but we feel we're beginning to accelerate. There's a sort of a J curve that is moving forward.[2] Once you have these partnering churches together, and people start to collaborate, I think the J curve can start to develop.

Conclusion. Jon has discovered that finding the right leaders is crucial both to enabling a big vision for a city and implementing a strategy that can facilitate that vision. He helpfully highlights that the leaders who can make this happen may not be the ones you'd expect. Not everyone who gets the idea can offer the time and energy needed to make it a reality, but gifted catalysts have a knack of finding leaders. They look for openings and opportunities, and they take them. As one author put it, "They meet people where they are. And in meeting people where they are, catalysts can inspire change without being coercive."[3]

Raising Up Leaders: Grace Church-Planting Network and the Samurai Project

An interview with Thierry Richards, lead planter of Marunouchi Church, Tokyo, and Samurai Projects director

Q. **Tell us a little about yourself and your city.**

A. **(Thierry)** My wife, Antonia, and three children live in central Tokyo. I have been working at Grace City Church Tokyo for eight years, alongside senior pastor Makoto Fukuda. The church was planted eight years ago and has grown numerically in a remarkable way for Japan—from 20 to 180 people in that time. We are thankful to the Lord. My wife and I are about to lead a church plant (Marunouchi Church Tokyo) into the center of the financial district of central Tokyo, an area called Marunouchi, near Tokyo Station.

Q. What makes Tokyo such a great city to live in?

A. One of the things I love about Tokyo is how punctual, efficient, and clean the public transport systems are. You can set your watch by what time the bus will arrive. If the chart says it will arrive at 0632, it will. If the trains are late by more than a minute, the conductor publicly apologizes to everybody for being late. And from Tokyo, you can get to many places in the country very easily by bullet trains, which are quick, quiet, and very comfortable.

Q. What are the particular challenges you face in a city like Tokyo?

A. Tokyo is the world's biggest city with a population of 35.9 million people. Yet just 0.3 percent are evangelical Christians. In contemporary Japanese churches, there is a famine of Bible-teaching, gospel-proclaiming laborers being raised up. Current churches can't find successors for elderly pastors, who may, therefore, continue into their nineties. There are not the people available for church planting. The result is a general decline in gospel witness throughout the country.

Q. What is your vision for Tokyo?

A. We desire that, under God, we can see ten new congregations started by 2020. So far we have seen five of those planted, four in the pipeline, and two other church planters at theological college. I would love to see a movement whereby people are confident in the mercies and provision of the Lord Jesus, such that they are willing to stand out from the crowd and speak about Jesus boldly and wisely with colleagues in their workplaces. If the seed of the gospel is scattered in this way through friendships in workplaces, some of the seed will bear fruit thirty, sixty, one hundredfold, causing many people to become Christians in Tokyo and in Japan. And along with this, I would love to see many of these new

Christians equipped to teach the Bible themselves, such that more and more Japanese get to learn about our Lord Jesus Christ and are rescued by him from the wrath to come on judgment day.

Q. How is it possible to think of a multiplication movement where the church is so small?

A. What is needed is a pipeline that will enable us to prioritize the raising up of the next generation of Bible-teaching servant leaders teaching the gospel of Jesus in the city of Tokyo and producing Christian communities. If we are to see multiplication, we need the engine to be servant-hearted gospel ministers.

Q. How is the Samurai Projects designed to help you achieve this goal?

A. First, on the name: the Japanese ideal of servanthood is called the Samurai code, and the national football team is called the Samurai Blues, so it seemed a good name to choose. The Samurai Projects is a program designed to help us raise up ten workers each year in contemporary Tokyo. We want to appoint them to the task of gospel proclamation, instruct them, and give them gospel-proclaiming opportunities and experience. This is for one or two years, doing full-time ministry from the platform of a church context. Upon graduating from the project, half will be sent out into the workplaces of Tokyo to proclaim the gospel there, as full-time business people, artists, and civil servants, and half will be sent into full-time church-planting and Bible-teaching work long term.

Q. How does the course work?

A. Three components make up the course:

1. *Training.* The participants are trained so they can teach the Bible to others. To do this, one afternoon a week, all the participants gather for a day of formal training. The participants

cover books of the Bible, such as Mark or Romans, in depth, as well as a Bible overview. They practice teaching these in a Bible-study format, and they receive feedback. Once a month, the participants also prepare a ten-minute Bible talk.

2. *Teaching.* The participants, the Samurai, are responsibility to lead a Bible-teaching ministry. For example, many of the Samurai lead a small-group Bible study, where they are required to read a Bible passage, understand what it is saying, and then prepare their own Bible study based on this passage and teach the passage to the small group they lead.

3. *Serving.* We believe that it's vital that each Samurai is trained in godliness and character by doing tasks to serve Tokyo and others in the church.

Q. How has it gone?

A. We were very excited to have ten participants for the first official year, 2016. Indeed, two candidates shared one place, so there were eleven Samurai doing ministry at three churches.

As we reflect on these early few years of the Samurai Projects, amid the challenges we have seen two church planters and three theological college students raised up, two Bible-teaching ministries started, and five church staff raised up. We are so thankful to our Lord Jesus Christ for starting, sustaining, and using this project.

Conclusion. There can't be many places tougher than Japan when it comes to attempting to develop an expansive church-planting program. It would be easy for leaders to complain about not having enough resources or people. But the Samurai Projects is a testimony to how to turn a weakness into an opportunity. If the need in Tokyo is to raise up leaders because they aren't going to come along on their own, there's a need to be strategic, intentional, and deliberate in work among the younger generation of the church. For some cities, collaborating in the raising up of workers is the beginning of the longer-term project of starting a church-planting movement.

Unity in Diversity: The Union Network of Churches in Pretoria, South Africa

An interview with Tobie Meyer, pastor of Ligpunt Church and network catalyst for City to City Africa

Q. Tell us about yourself.

A. **(Tobie)** I'm married to Mariana, and we are raising three daughters in Pretoria, South Africa. I am one of the pastors at Ligpunt, a church I helped plant in 2010. I also oversee the work of City to City Africa, which seeks to catalyze church-planting movements in the leading cities of sub-Saharan Africa.

Q. Tell us something about your city.

A. As the capital, Pretoria has always been at the center of South Africa's colorful political history. It imprisoned the likes of Winston Churchill and Mahatma Gandhi, but also made Nelson Mandela president. It also has the fastest-growing population of any South African city.

Q. What is God doing in and through the Union in Pretoria?

A. The Union is the fruit of an organic work that the Lord seems to have been doing over some years in bringing friends together from various backgrounds. Even before the first of the churches was planted in 2010, relationships were building between churches and ministries that had a kingdom-minded desire to see others flourish. Here are some of the ingredients that contributed to this:

1. *Catalysts.* External catalytic influences of church-planting networks (like Acts 29 and City to City) drew like-minded local leaders together around a common vision.

2. *Conviction.* This strengthened the conviction that our city needs the gospel and that church planting is the most effective way to drive that gospel into every corner of the city through diverse plants that reach different subcultures.

3. *Training.* A training partnership was formed on the premise that planters will need to be equipped but that we can do so more effectively when we play to each other's strengths and acknowledge we can learn from each other.

Q. **How has church culture enabled collaboration to happen?**

A. A younger generation of ministers has emerged who feel relatively little obligation to older institutional (denominational and political) boundaries. In many ways they are trustingly and generously supported by institutions in many cases, but at the same time, they are being exposed (through technology, travel, and immigration) to global best practice in collaborative church planting. All of this has meant they feel free and have been given the room to experiment and innovate.

Q. **What has excited you about the extent of partnership that you have been a part of in Pretoria?**

A. The Union has been able to bring together a huge spectrum of socially and racially diverse planters into a network. Even though it's still in its infancy, it really does reflect something of the diversity of the city we've been called to reach.

A couple of things are worth commenting on: First, some of us live in and minister in contexts with no electricity and running water while others reach influential national government, business, and cultural leaders. This means some of our churches worship only in African languages, and others mix it up. It means two churches in the network may target individuals on the opposite extremes of the political spectrum with the same gospel. It means when we gather together to worship as a network, not yet all but many of the tribes and tongues and nations that call Pretoria home bow before the same Lord and reach out to each other as brothers and sisters. So, there really is a precious unity in our diversity.

Second, our unity is fragile but for the Lord's continuing grace to us. The unity is readily threatened by external cultural forces (our nation wrestles with racial and economic inequality in a polarizing way, constantly suggesting we should align ourselves with "our people"—whatever that is conveniently defined as) and our own internal lingering prejudices.

Q. So, what do you think has made it work?

A. These things stand out in my mind:

1. Everyone has a heart for all the people of Pretoria and would love to see them reached with the gospel. As a result, there is a thorough understanding that we need each other.

2. This is coupled with a robust commitment to contextualization for the sake of reaching into the different segments of society and culture with the same gospel.

3. The Union has a flat leadership structure. Our history has often meant that someone is given a seat at the table either as a second-class member or as a token gesture. Through no design of our own, the network is led by a group of men who highly value each other as peers. The one downside to this is that it can be difficult to make decisions.

4. There exists deep trust among the leaders.

5. That deep trust is a function of time spent together.

6. We have an eagerness to understand each other and learn from each other as God's gift to us and a willingness to acknowledge

our blindness to our cultural prejudice and as a result each
other's joy and pain.

7. There is a <u>readiness to repent quickly</u> when we get it wrong, as
we often do.

8. We seek to share resources and proximity that make it possible
to, for instance, have a <u>number of churches share the same
office space.</u>

Q. Any final thoughts?

A. All of this really is the fruit of the gospel. The gospel has done and
continues to do its work of humbling the hearts of men and
women on the one hand, and on the other has given them a vision
of the kingdom that is richer than any one church on its own
could ever do justice.

Conclusion. How do we overcome fears or mistrust that inhibit
collaboration when we are working across class or cultural barriers,
especially where there is also a history of racial inequality or prejudice?
The story of the Pretoria network is one of the power of the gospel to
overcome inertia and to bring extremely diverse planters together into
meaningful partnership.

Perhaps two lessons stand out from the work in Pretoria. First, it's
essential that a collaborative movement truly functions as a peer-to-peer
initiative. Unless there is a genuinely flat leadership structure in
which everyone has an equal voice around the table, it's unlikely to
hold together. That is not easy to pull off.

Second, experience suggests that the gifts and abilities of the catalytic
leader(s) is key to the chances of a diverse movement working. When
facilitating relationships among a wide range of planters, catalysts need
to be high on emotional intelligence: able to connect and bond with
people from very different backgrounds. They also need to exemplify the
sacrificial and self-giving attitude that is the heart of the movement.

Perseverance: Hamburg Project in Hamburg, Germany

An interview with Daniel Bartz, pastor of Hamburgprojekt, Foundation of the Free Evangelical Churches in Northern Germany (FeGN)

Q. Tell us a bit about yourself and the city you serve.

A. **(Daniel)** I'm married to Kathrine, and we have three cute little girls. We planted a church ten years ago in Germany's second-largest city. Approximately two million in the city and five million in the metro area call Hamburg their home. It has a vibrant music culture (the Beatles made it here), a large trade hub, and a center for Germany's creative industry. It is expected to grow by two hundred thousand people in the next thirty years. Let alone the numbers, we would love to plant enough churches to reach 1 percent of its population. Through the church-planting network, we are building up with different denominations and tribes, and that number must be increased.

Q. Do you think it's possible to build collaborative church-planting movements in the cities of Europe?

A. A few years ago, we had a City to City conference in Lisbon, Portugal. The book *Center Church* had just come out. I remember that one of the local leaders responded to this massive piece of church-planting expertise with "It's not that easy, Tim."

In most regards, he is right. Church planting on continental post-Christian Europe is a hard job and not very fruitful; it takes a long time. This is not America. This is not Asia. You need perseverance for planting a single church—and certainly for creating a church-planting network in your city or even in your region. Many churches are small. They don't have a vision for their city, but rather have a castle mentality. Churches are internally focused and divided among themselves because all too often the emphasis is on differences rather than similarities.

And when it comes to the majority of people living in the big cities of Europe, a friend of mine put it like this: "People forgot that they forgot about God."

Q. So, it's been tough at times?

A. Yes! We launched our first daughter church after five years. We had the church planter in training for two years and were full of excitement sending him to plant. Four years later, we had to close that church plant due to some personal issues and the planter's lack of leadership. We are glad we could take over most of the people, but the church plant failed.

The church planter of our second daughter church in the city became seriously sick with clinical depression, and we had to call off the plant. Another daughter plant in Istanbul and one in Hamburg are going very slowly. Through all of this, we've really had to learn to persevere.

Q. But you have persevered?

A. With the sending of our first planter about five years ago, we started to meet with him, training, coaching, and praying. Out of that meeting, a little network emerged. First it was just us and our daughter planters. Later we invited befriended planters in the city—lots of relational work. One day the board of the Evangelical Alliance in our city asked our little network to lead and coordinate all church-planting initiatives in the whole city.

Connecting, building relationships, helping, dreaming, praying. We went from five to about fifteen represented plants. But even fifteen won't change the city.

Q. And for the future?

A. Just recently we developed a vision for our city for church planting. "Planting together!" Christians in Hamburg have a joint spiritual responsibility for our city. We have a common concern to reach the people with the grace and love of God and to renew the city with the gospel. We believe that we need new churches to reach new people groups and newcomers to the city. We want to see a movement planting all different kinds of churches for reaching varieties of people with the gospel.

How are we going to do this?

1. *Training.* Find, promote, assess, and coach new planters together.
2. *Strategic work.* Pray, identify less-reached neighborhoods and milieus, sharing resources, having a common strategy for the city together.
3. *Network.* Strengthen and accompany existing churches to win them for church planting together.

Q. **What is the biggest challenge in seeing a movement for your city?**

A. I must admit that this is only going to happen with Jesus' blessing and with new planters. This is by far the greatest need. And that's why we will start with a church-planting training center in early 2019, for creating greater awareness for new planters with a full-blown training along with assessment and coaching. This is also going to be in partnership with a similar center in Frankfurt to eventually create training for the whole region and Europe. We are excited and looking forward to what God is going to do.

Q. **What words of advice do you have for someone thinking of attempting to start a collaborative movement in their own city?**

A. God is faithful. That's our biggest lesson learned. Even with setbacks and hard circumstances, we still have a calling to plant churches in our cities, in the region, in Europe. With a constantly renewed and refreshed faith, with lots of prayer, with patience and humbleness, with a kingdom mindset, with perseverance, and with God's blessing we are planting more churches in Europe.

Conclusion. The Hamburg story demonstrates that sometimes the biggest challenge in ministry is not to lose heart when the going gets tough. Planting brings with it more than its fair share of risk. But this story encourages us that we should not be afraid to fail. Setbacks are very often crucial learning opportunities. They can be the very thing that makes us as they offer new insights: what worked, what didn't, what could be done differently, and so on. And taken this way, setbacks help to develop resilience as we persevere.

Summary

What have we learned from our whistle-stop tour of the world? What are the commonalities across these examples?

First, only a Spirit-inspired kingdom culture can bring people together and keep them together, especially when they come from such diverse backgrounds. If spiritual movements are to happen *at all* in our cities, God must be at work. A big idea and a grand vision may be enough to create some superficial interest, but we overlook the need for fervent prayer at our peril.

Second, catalytic leadership needs to be better understood because it plays a unique and crucial role in facilitating a movement. Catalytic leaders take a genuine interest in people over projects, desire to bless and to serve, bring out the best in what they find, and promote the interests of the movement above their own. Strangely but appropriately, these people are often humble and self-effacing. They are unlikely to put themselves forward but must be encouraged to do so.

Finally, building a collaborative movement for your city requires you to be highly adaptable. You will depend on who God raises up, who God brings along, what role they can play, and how much time they can give. This is going to look different in every city. In both church planting and movement building, context is key. These diverse contexts demonstrate that whatever the complexities, it's possible to find a way to be together for the city.

Conclusion

No man is an island, entire of itself;

every man is a piece of the continent, a part of the main;

if a clod be washed away by the sea, Europe is the less, as well as if a

promontory were, as well as any manner of thy friends or of thine

own were; any man's death diminishes me, because I am involved

in mankind. And therefore never send to know

for whom the bell tolls; it tolls for thee.

JOHN DONNE

I (John) switched off the TV and allowed the reality of what I had just watched sink in. A couple from our church had just been interviewed on *Midlands Today*, our regional news program, because after many years of a crippling spiral of debts, they were finally free.

Look around them, and you will see that I have had very little to do with helping them in this. It's way beyond my expertise. They were supported by a charity called Christians Against Poverty (CAP), and in particular one CAP center manager, who lives around the corner from us and who has worked closely with them to clear their debts and begin to budget properly.

Zoom out a little further, and you'll see that the creation of that CAP center began when three churches that belonged to 2020birmingham talked together about how they could establish this kind of mercy ministry in Birmingham. Since then, a number of churches beyond 2020birmingham have also begun to join the collaboration and support the CAP center.

Widen the angle again, and you'll see that the couple in question had come to faith through outreach clubs we run as a church. Over the course of the past two years, they had been figuring out what it means to make Jesus the Lord of every area of their lives. Their progress in this area is an amazing testimony to the grace of God.

Pan out further still, and you'll see that this man and his wife are the most fantastic evangelists in our local area. She is a hairdresser in the community and so has a captive audience; she talks to her clients about the gospel. "It's happened again, John," she will say. "I don't know how, but we just got talking about Jesus." Her husband serves in our community coffee morning and is currently being trained in a variety of ways to be more effective in the ministry God has clearly gifted him for. We're working out together what it may mean for him to be Crossway Church's first ministry apprentice with a focus on evangelism. The prayer for indigenous leadership is becoming a reality—by the grace of God.

A Movement of Movements

This is just a tiny glimpse of what we're beginning to see happen in small pockets around the city and what we long to see spread with real vitality across Birmingham and the wider region. What we long to see is a movement of robust and healthy church-planting churches collaborating to see sweeter unity, more fervent prayer gatherings, more effective evangelism, compassionate and tailored mercy ministries, faith and work initiatives, and anything else that may happen, within a gospel ecosystem where churches are genuinely discovering what it means to be together for the city.

Tim Keller wrote,

> Every city in the world needs Jesus Christ. But our cities do not merely need a few more churches and ministries here and there; they need gospel city movements that lead to citywide tipping points. So urban ministers enthusiastically and passionately give their lives to see these goals, even though they may not see their consummation in their own lifetimes.[1]

The goal is a movement of movements, a gospel ecosystem seeking citywide impact. In Birmingham, we believe we're beginning to see the culture change, if only in small ways. It's remarkable how much more willing churches are to collaborate on real projects. Recently an evangelistic event exploring the relationship between science and Christianity took over the Town Hall in the city center. It was a significant collaboration between a number of churches within 2020birmingham and a number of other churches and parachurch organizations that joined to make it happen. As a result, nine hundred people gathered to hear a world-class speaker address the question of whether science and Christianity mix. Not only that, but leading up to the event, local churches gathered to be trained in follow-up relationship evangelism for those who attended.

We have both been struck how the tone of the conversation around church planting has changed in certain circles. In chapter two, Neil described sitting in a meeting with the Midlands Gospel Partnership, a regional coalition of conservative evangelical churches in 2009, and realizing that no one in the room had any intention of planting. Just a few months ago, we both sat in the same room with the same church leaders and were amazed by the way they were beginning to believe that church planting was both necessary and possible. Not only that, but they were exploring how it may be possible to begin an equivalent of 2020birmingham in their own locality.

Increasingly, others from further afield are looking in and wondering what it may mean for them to be together for their city. Stephan Pues, director of City to City Europe, stated, "I see how Birmingham has become an inspiring example of leaders and city movements all over Europe. 2020birmingham leaders from different denominations and backgrounds don't build their own kingdoms, but together they serve God's kingdom in their city."

But how does it begin?

Tamzine and The Regal Lady

We began this book by raising the alarm. The bell tolls for us. The urgency of this present age requires us to launch lifeboats. The mistake would be to believe that the best strategy to answer the alarm would be a single, sleek vessel, an ecclesiastical *QE2*, that would single-handedly, effortlessly glide to victory.

No, this is a Dunkirk moment, calling for a Dunkirk spirit as we pray for a Dunkirk miracle. How can we work together for the city? We are, by nature, dependent creatures. As Christians, we confess as much in the sight of God. "Unless the LORD builds the house, the builders labor in vain" (Psalm 127:1). And what about our dependence on each other? No one is an island.

In a corner of the Imperial War Museum in London sits a small wooden fishing boat named *Tamzine*. It's 14 feet and 7.5 inches long, open, and the smallest vessel to sail in Dunkirk. It surely seems inadequate for the task. However, people were saved from certain death because *Tamzine* played its part.

I (John) grew up in the Yorkshire seaside down of Scarborough. If you ever have the privilege of visiting, you must take a boat trip from the harbor up and down the coastline. One particular vessel still offers such excursions. It's a steel pleasure steamer built in the 1930s, originally powered by coal and later converted to diesel. It isn't particularly impressive, with plenty of patches of rust and a need for a lick of paint.

But this vessel, like *Tamzine*, took part in Operation Dynamo. As unimpressive as it may appear, it carried twelve hundred troops in three crossings over the English Channel from Dunkirk back to Ramsgate. Its name is *The Regal Lady*.

Friends, what will it take for us to be regal ladies and gentlemen? How will we lead our churches into becoming regal? Do we believe with John Donne that "any man's death diminishes" us? This is not about our size or our material condition. It's about our fidelity, urgency, compassion, generosity, and humility. When we come together for the city, who knows what good will come of it and what God might do?

Together for the City

The Lord Jesus Christ prays for his disciples, and then he prays for *us*

> that all of them may be one, Father, just as you are in me and I am in you. May they also be in us so that the world may believe that you have sent me. I have given them the glory that you gave me, that they may be one as we are one—I in them and you in me—so that they may be brought to complete unity. Then the world will know that you sent me and have loved them even as you have loved me. (John 17:21-23)

Jesus prays that our unity will convince the world that his claim that he is the supreme revelation of God is true. But it's more than that. It is, as theologian D. A. Carson put it, "breathtakingly extravagant." Our unity is a sign that we have "been caught up into the love of the Father for the Son, secure and content, and fulfilled because loved by the Almighty himself, with the very same love he reserves for his Son. It is hard to imagine a more compelling evangelistic appeal."[2]

May Jesus' prayer be our prayer. May we be so caught up in the love of the Father that we are released from the shackles of tribalism. May we be so renewed by the justifying work of the Son that we have nothing left to prove. May we be so filled with his Holy Spirit that we are empowered to realize a bigger vision, for the sake of lost men and women and the kingdom of God. "May the God who gives endurance and encouragement give you the same attitude of mind toward each other that Christ Jesus had, so that with one mind and one voice we may glorify the God and Father of our Lord Jesus Christ" (Romans 15:5-6).

Acknowledgments

Together we would like to especially thank Brandon O'Brien at City to City, who has given so much thought and care to this project and so much support and encouragement to us. We would also like to thank those at City to City who have been kind enough to engage with this project, in particular Tim Keller, Al Barth, and Mark Reynolds. Very special thanks must go to all of our colaborers at 2020birmingham, especially Angela Morah and Alex Robinson, who work so hard behind the scenes. Thank you, Jonathan Bell, Andy Weatherley, Jo Weatherley, Jez Dearing, Colin Tamplin, Barnaby Pain, Ro Pain, John Walley, Abraham Belew, Kenny Dubnick, and Hilary Lynch for contributing content for the book. Thanks also to Patricio Oyarzún, Jon Dennis, Thierry Richards, Tobie Meyer, and Daniel Bartz for your invaluable case studies. Finally, thank you to our friends at IVP, in particular Al Hsu, who has overseen this project from beginning to end.

● —— ● —— ●

Neil recognizes that there are many he would like to honor for making this book possible:

To my family I owe more than can be said in words. My wife, Jane, and our children, Rufus and Felix, are a constant source of encouragement even when I ask of them more than is ever fair.

To Mum and Dad, thanks for the nurture and care of a loving home that helped make me who I am.

To special friends Mike and Rachel du Plessis so much is owed. They not only introduced me to the Lord through their witness but then introduced me to my wife, and without their rich generosity down the years 2020birmingham could never have thrived in the way it has.

Redeemer City to City is the reason we have a story to tell. Thanks to Al Barth for first taking a risk in inviting me to connect with City to City, and then for his constant encouragement and counsel over many years. Thanks are also due to Tim Keller, whose vision for cities and gospel collaboration is the inspiration for our endeavors.

To all at City Church who have let me travel and speak on countless occasions over the past twenty years. To John and Ursula Stevens and Hugh Thomson for planting a church together—thanks for an amazing journey.

To my PA, Angela Morah—what can be said other than that time and again you keep the train from coming off the tracks through your care and dedication.

To Jonathan Bell, without whose generosity, humility, vision, and dedication the story would never have begun. What started as a tentative partnership has become a lasting friendship.

To my coauthor, John—anyone who has seen this book develop knows it was only his monumental effort that ensured a good idea ever saw the light of day.

●—●—●

John would like to personally thank his family. Without your patience, understanding, and sacrifice this book would not have been written.

Notes

Introduction: The Bigger Picture

[1]Macmillan nurses are specialists that offer palliative care to cancer patients.
[2]The traveling community in the United Kingdom is an itinerant group of predominantly Irish descent. They are pejoratively referred to as gypsies. A hostel is a particular type of short-term accommodation for people with no home.
[3]The closest equivalent in the United States to a UK council estate is a public housing project.

1 Vision

[1]Peter Brierley, *UK Church Statistics* 3 (Tonbridge, UK: ADBC Publishers, 2018), 0.2, 4.

[2]Jason Mandryk, *Operation World*, 7th ed. (Colorado Springs, CO: Biblica Publishing, 2010), 852.

[3]Mandryk, *Operation World*, 74-75.

[4]R. Albert Mohler Jr., "Christ Will Build and Rebuild His Church" in Mohler, *A Guide to Church Revitalization* (Louisville, KY: SBTS Press, 2015), 7.

[5]"The Birmingham Economic Review 2017: Population and Employment," University of Birmingham, accessed Jan 28, 2019, https://blog.bham.ac.uk/cityredi /the-birmingham-economic-review-2017-population-and-employment.

[6]In 2011 the five UK cities with a population of more than one-fifth Muslims were Luton (24 percent), Slough (23 percent), Blackburn (27 percent), Bradford (25 percent), and Birmingham (22 percent). "2011 Census: Religion, local authorities in England and Wales" (xls). United Kingdom Census 2011. Office for National Statistics. Accessed Jan 28, 2019, www.ons.gov.uk/ons/rel/census/2011-census/key-statistics-for-local -authorities-in-england-and-wales/rft-table-ks209ew.xls.

[7]Peter Brierley, *UK Church Statistics 2, 2010-2020* (Tonbridge, UK: ADBC Publishers, 2014), sect. 13.1.4.

[8]See Daniel C. Timmer, *A Gracious and Compassionate God* (Downers Grove, IL: InterVarsity Press, 2011), 32-37.

[9]For example see David Garrison, *Church Planting Movements* (Richmond, VA: International Mission Board, 2015), 7. PDF at www.call2all.org /wp-content/uploads/2015/12/Church_Planting_Movements_Garrison.pdf.

[10] J. C. Ryle, *Matthew* (Edinburgh: Banner of Truth Trust, 2012), 57.

[11] Timothy J. Keller, *Center Church* (Grand Rapids: Zondervan, 2012), 46.

[12] Paraphrase of Gary Keller, *The One Thing* (London: John Murray, 2013), 89.

[13] Paraphrase of Keller, *The One Thing*, 91.

[14] David Platt, "Our Obligation to the Unreached," Desiring God, December 26, 2014, www.desiringgod.org/articles/our-obligation-to-the-unreached.

[15] Platt, "Our Obligation to the Unreached."

[16] Platt, "Our Obligation to the Unreached."

[17] Platt, "Our Obligation to the Unreached."

[18] David Platt, "Our Obligation to the Unreached," Desiring God, December 26, 2014, www.desiringgod.org/articles/our-obligation-to-the-unreached.

[19] David Goodhart, *The Road to Somewhere* (London: Penguin, 2017), vii.

[20] Goodhart, *The Road to Somewhere*, 37.

[21] Goodhart, *The Road to Somewhere*, xv.

[22] Martin Charlesworth and Natalie Williams, *A Church for the Poor* (Eastbourne, UK: David C Cook UK, 2017), 69. This statistic is taken from a YouGov survey in 2014.

[23] Charlesworth and Williams, *A Church for the Poor*, 69. This statistic is taken from research in 2015.

[24] We are indebted to David Shaw, Oak Hill College, who in conversation drew our attention to the way these two 9:38s relate to each other. He has recently written a reflection on this in *Commentary*, Summer 2018, a publication of Oak Hill College, Southgate, London.

[25] See James Edwards, *Mark* (Leicester, UK: Apollos, 2002), 290.

[26] David Shaw, "What Kind of Workers?" in *Commentary*, Summer 2018, Oak Hill College, 27.

[27] J. C. Ryle, *Mark* (Edinburgh: The Banner of Truth Trust, 2012), 151.

[28] Frank S. Thielman, *Philippians: The NIV Application Commentary Book* (Grand Rapids: Zondervan, 1995), 62.

[29] Markus Bockmuehl, *The Epistle to the Philippians*, Black's New Testament Commentaries (London: A&C Black, 1997), 80.

[30] Gordon Fee, *Paul's Letter to the Philippians*, New International Commentary on the New Testament (Grand Rapids: Eerdmans, 1995), 125.

[31] Frank S. Theilman, *Philippians: The NIV Application Commentary Book* (Grand Rapids: Zondervan, 1995), 66.

[32] This is a variation of a *very* old joke. Apologies if it made you groan. Please be assured that no church planters were harmed during the writing of this book.

[33]See Daniel Yang, "The Need for Multi-Denominational Church Planting Networks in Our Cities," *Christianity Today*, September 5, 2017, www.christianity today.com/edstetzer/2017/september/need-for-multi-denominational-church -planting-networks-in-o.html.

2 Beginnings

[1]Niall Ferguson, *The Square and the Tower* (London: Penguin, 2018), 30, 33.

[2]A ministry established by Shari Thomas and Tami Resch that provides gospel coaching, training, and network development for spouses in church planting. See www.parakaleo.us.

[3]Ferguson, *The Square and the Tower*, 47.

3 Movements

[1]Alan Hirsch, "Reflections on Movement Dynamics," in Timothy Keller, *Serving a Movement* (Grand Rapids: Zondervan, 2016), 253 (emphasis his).

[2]Timothy J. Keller, *Center Church* (Grand Rapids: Zondervan, 2012), 337.

[3]At this stage, we will be leaning on a number of key insights from a chapter entitled "Movements and Institutions" in Keller's *Center Church*. We are road-testing these dynamic with 2020birmingham, and they are confirmed by the experiences of other city movements, examples of which appear later in this book.

[4]Keller, *Center Church*, 340.

[5]Keller, *Center Church*, 340.

[6]Roy Clements, *The Strength of Weakness* (Fearn, UK: Christian Focus Publications, 1994), 178.

[7]Ed Stetzer and Warren Bird, *Viral Churches: Helping Church Planters Become Movement Makers* (San Francisco: Jossey-Bass, 2010), 178-79.

[8]Danile Kewley and Sven Östring, "Can Church Planting Movements Emerge in the West? Case Studies of Three Church Planting Strategies in Western Australia," *Journal of Adventist Mission Studies*, 2010, 2:25-43, 28.

[9]Keller, *Center Church*, 337.

[10]Lesslie Newbigin, *The Gospel in a Pluralist Society* (London: SPCK, 1989), 116 (italics ours).

[11]Hirsch, "Reflections," 256.

[12]Hirsch, "Reflections," 256.

[13]Stetzer and Bird, *Viral Churches*, 143.

[14]Keller, *Center Church*, 339.

[15]Kewley and Östring, "Can Church Planting Movements Emerge," 33-34.

[16]See Graham Beynon, *Planting for the Gospel* (Fearn, UK: Christian Focus Publications, 2011), chap. 2.

[17]These dynamics are similar to those discussed in the chapter "Movements and Institutions" in Keller's *Center Church*.

[18]For a look at how globalization affects business and also lifestyles in general, see Binyamin Appelbaum, "Perils of Globalization," *New York Times*, May 17, 2015, www.nytimes.com/2015/05/18/business/a-decade-later-loss-of-maytag-factory -still-resonates.html.

[19]See Chris Bruno and Matt Dirks, *Churches Partnering Together: Biblical Strategies for Fellowship, Evangelism, and Compassion* (Wheaton, IL: Crossway, 2014).

[20]Bruno and Dirks, *Churches Partnering Together*, 40.

[21]Daniel Yang, *The Need For Multi-Denominational Church Planting Networks in Our Cities*, Christianity Today International, September 5, 2015, www.christianitytoday.com/edstetzer/2017/september/need-for-multi -denominational-church-planting-networks-in-o.html.

[22]David E. Garland, *1 Corinthians* (Grand Rapids: Baker Academic, 2003), 112.

[23]Matt Perman, *What's Best Next* (Grand Rapids: Zondervan, 2014), 229.

[24]For more information about church revitalization, we encourage you to read John James, *Renewal: Church Revitalization along the Way of the Cross* (Leyland, UK: 10 Publishing, 2016).

[25]Niall Ferguson, *The Square and the Tower* (London: Penguin, 2017), 425.

[26]Ferguson, *The Square and the Tower*, 430 (our italics).

[27]See Ferguson, *The Square and the Tower*, 47.

[28]See Keller, *Center Church*, 344.

4 Core

[1]Cambridge Dictionary, "Dunkirk spirit," https://dictionary.cambridge.org /dictionary/english/dunkirk-spirit.

[2]Dale T. Miller, "Why Social Movements Should Favor Collaboration over Confrontation," Stanford Business, May 21, 2015, www.gsb.stanford.edu /insights/why-social-movements-should-favor-collaboration-over -confrontation.

[3]Jeff Liu and Paul Brody, "Is Collaboration the New Innovation?," *Harvard Business Review*, 2016, https://hbr.org/resources/pdfs/comm /ey/IsCollaborationTheNewInnovation.pdf.

[4]We appreciate that the term *evangelical* can be open to more than one interpretation, and that the boundaries of evangelicalism are at times contested. To understand what we believe to be core evangelical beliefs, you can access the 2020birmingham statement of faith at www.2020birmingham .org/about/statement-of-faith.php.

[5]Barnes, in Philip Graham Ryken, *Galatians* (Phillipsburg, NJ: P&R Publishing, 2005), 47.

[6]Ryken, *Galatians*, 47-48.

[7]For example, see the basis of Churches Together in England: www.cte.org.uk /Groups/234695/Home/About/Basis_of_CTE/Basis_of_CTE.aspx.

[8]The terms *foundation* and *focus* as a way of describing this relationship are taken from Chris Bruno and Matt Dirks, *Churches Partnering Together: Biblical Strategies for Fellowship, Evangelism, and Compassion* (Wheaton, IL: Crossway, 2014).

5 Cause

[1]See Together for the Gospel's website at http://t4g.org/about/ for further details.

[2]See the Gospel Coalition's website at www.thegospelcoalition.org/about/ for further details.

[3]Chris Bruno and Matt Dirks, *Churches Partnering Together: Biblical Strategies for Fellowship, Evangelism, and Compassion* (Wheaton, IL: Crossway, 2014), 33.

[4]Bruno and Dirks, *Churches Partnering Together*, 36.

[5]See Timothy Keller, *Center Church* (Grand Rapids: Zondervan, 2012), 18.

[6]Michael Felker, "Do You Have a Theological Vision?," Kicking at the Darkness, December 13, 2012, www.michealfelker.com/do-you-have-a -theological-vision/.

[7]Keller, *Center Church*, 21.

[8]Keller, *Center Church*, 18.

[9]See Daniel Strange, "For Their Rock Is Not as Our Rock: The Gospel as the 'Subversive Fulfillment' of the Religious Other," www.etsjets.org/files /JETS-PDFs/56/56-2/JETS_56-2_379-395_Strange.pdf, 379-95. His 2015 book, *Their Rock Is Not as Our Rock: A Theology of Religions*, is available through Zondervan. Dan himself attributes the phase "subversive fulfillment" to the Dutch missiologist Hendrik Kraemer.

[10]From Tim Chester and Steve Timmis, *Everyday Church* (Nottingham, UK: Inter-Varsity Press, 2011), 21-22.

[11]Keller, *Center Church*, 21.

6 Code

[1] Alan Hirsch, "Reflections on Movement Dynamics," in Keller, *Serving a Movement* (Grand Rapids: Zondervan, 2016), 262.

[2] Tom Wright explores this example in *Paul for Everyone: Galatians and Thessalonians* (London: SPCK, 2002), 28.

[3] Jordan Peterson, *12 Rules for Life* (London: Penguin Allen Lane, 2018), 337.

[4] Peterson, *12 Rules for Life*, 337.

[5] David Wells, *Turning to God* (Grand Rapids: Baker Books, 1989), 169.

[6] Tim Chester, *Titus for You* (London: The Good Book Company, 2014), 12.

[7] Mark Dever, *9 Marks of a Healthy Church* (Wheaton, IL: Crossway, 2004), 15.

[8] Ed Stetzer and Daniel Im, *Planting Missional Churches* 2nd ed. (Nashville: B&H Academic, 2016), 42.

[9] Timothy Keller, "Why Plant Churches?," n.p., PDF at http://download.redeemer.com/pdf/learn/resources/Why_Plant_Churches-Keller.pdf.

[10] Ed Stetzer and Warren Bird, *Viral Churches* (San Francisco: Jossey-Bass, 2010), 25.

[11] See North American Mission Board, June 14, 2018, "NAMB SBC Report: Ezell spotlights Disciple-Making Task Force, Church Planting Impact," https://www.namb.net/news/namb-sbc-report-ezell-spotlights-disciple-making-task-force-church-planting-impact/.

[12] Keller, *Center Church*, 356-57.

[13] Peter Brierley, *UK Church Statistics No. 3: 2018* (Tonbridge, UK: ADBC Publishers, 2017), 16.1, 5.

[14] Brierley, *UK Church Statistics*, 16.1, 5.

[15] Brierley, *UK Church Statistics*, 16.1, 5.

[16] Brierley, *UK Church Statistics*, 16.1, 5, says 1,143 opened, 1,737 closed. The net difference is negative 594.

[17] Anglican, Baptist, Methodist, and United Reformed churches all report declining numbers of churches.

[18] Winston Churchill, *The World Crisis 1911-1918* (London: Penguin Books, 2007) vol. 3, pt. 1, 140.

[19] Gary Keller, *The One Thing* (London: John Murray, 2013), 122.

[20] Keller, *The One Thing*, 87.

[21] Eckhard J. Schnabel, *Early Christian Mission*, vol. 2 (Downers Grove, IL: InterVarsity Press, 2004), 1480-81.

[22] J.C. Ryle, *Luke*, vol. 1. (Edinburgh: The Banner of Truth Trust, 2012), 143.

[23]Ed Stetzer and Warren Bird, *Viral Churches* (San Francisco: Wiley, 2010), 108.

[24]Patrick Lencioni, *The Advantage* (San Francisco: Jossey-Bass, 2012), 54.

[25]Keller, *The One Thing*, 118, 204.

[26]See John Ortberg, "Category Confusion," Christianity Today, www
.christianitytoday.com/pastors/2010/june-online-only/categoryconfusion.html.

[27]For a discussion of this, see Jonathan Leeman, "The Logical Fallacy of
Centered-Set Churches," 9Marks, June 12, 2014, www.9marks.org/article
/the-logical-fallacy-of-centered-set-churches/.

[28]Adapted from Hiebert 1994, 112, cited by Rupen Das, "Becoming a Follower
of Christ: Exploring Conversion Through Historical and Missiological
Lenses," International Baptist Theological Study Center & Vrije Universiteit,
Amsterdam, www.researchgate.net/publication/324609649_Becoming_a
_Follower_of_Christ_Exploring_Conversion_Through_Historical_and
_Missiological_Lenses.

7 Collaboration

[1]Mark Anderson, "Why Do Some Clouds Rain and Others Don't?," *New
Scientist*, January 26, 2008, 45.

[2]Figure taken from Snow Crystals, "Snowflake Science," accessed January 4,
2019, www.snowcrystals.com/science/science.html.

[3]From Henry David Thoreau's journal, dated January 5, 1856. Accessed online
at https://hdt.typepad.com/henrys_blog/2012/01/january-5-1856.html.

[4]At this point, we're leaning heavily on the approach of triperspectivalism as
advocated by John Frame. For example, see John Frame, *The Doctrine of the
Christian Life* (Phillipsburg, NJ: P&R Publishing, 2008), 33-37.

8 Taking Part

[1]The digitized editions of Commons and Lords Hansard, the Official Report
of debates in Parliament, is available online. The speech can be accessed in
full at https://api.parliament.uk/historic-hansard/commons/1940/jun/18
/war-situation. See specifically 60-61.

[2]The digitized editions of Commons and Lords Hansard, the Official
Report of debates in Parliament is available online. The speech can be accessed in full here. See specifically 1362-1365. https://api.parliament.uk
/historic-hansard/commons/1940/may/08/conduct-of-the-war.

[3]Terry Virgo, *The Tide Is Turning* (Chichester, UK: New Wine Ministries,
2006), 123.

[4]Jim C. Collins, *Good to Great* (London: Random House, 2001), 28.

[5]Chris Bruno and Matt Dirks, *Churches Partnering Together: Biblical Strategies for Fellowship, Evangelism, and Compassion* (Wheaton, IL: Crossway, 2014), 139.

[6]Bruno and Dirks, *Churches Partnering Together,* 148.

[7]Bruno and Dirks, *Churches Partnering Together,* 137.

[8]One assessment tool is Lifeway's Church Planter Candidate Assessment at http://churchplanter.lifeway.com/.

[9]Scott Thomas and Tom Wood, *Gospel Coach* (Grand Rapids: Zondervan, 2012), 23.

[10]Colin Marshall and Tony Payne, *The Trellis and the Vine* (Kingsford NSW: Matthias Media, 2009), 7-15.

[11]Alan Hirsch, *The Forgotten Ways* (Grand Rapids: Baker Books, 2006), 194.

[12]Collins, *Good to Great,* 121.

[13]Timothy Keller, *Serving a Movement* (Grand Rapids: Zondervan, 2016), 201.

[14]J. I. Packer, *A Passion for Faithfulness* (Wheaton, IL: Crossway, 1995), 131.

[15]See Adrian Reynolds, *Teaching Ezra* (Fearn, UK: Christian Focus Publications, 2018), 99-100.

[16]See Charles Handy, *The Age of Paradox* (Cambridge, MA: Harvard Business School Press, 1994), 49-67.

[17]John White, quoted in Packer, *A Passion for Faithfulness,* 125.

9 Together Around the World

[1]See this and more at Redeemer City to City, "Equipping Leaders to Develop Church Planters in Chicago," April 11, 2017, www.redeemercitytocity .com/blog/2017/4/11/equipping-leaders-to-develop-church-planters-in -chicago.

[2]A J curve depicts exponential logarithmic growth.

[3]Ori Brafman and Rod A. Beckstrom, *The Starfish and the Spider* (New York: Penguin, 2006), 124.

Conclusion

[1]Timothy Keller, *Center Church* (Grand Rapids: Zondervan, 2012), 377.

[2]D. A. Carson, *The Gospel According to John* (Grand Rapids: Eerdmans, 1991), 569.

2020birmingham

Church planting in Birmingham since 2010

1. *Crossway Church*, revitalisation (2010)
2. *Churchcentral West*, multi-site (2010)
3. *Real life Church*, pioneer (2011)
4. *OIKOS Community Church*, pioneer (2011)
5. *Churchcentral North*, multi-site (2012)
6. *Emmaus Church*, pioneer (2012)
7. *Ethiopian Evangelical Church*, pioneer (2012)
8. *Bearwood Chapel*, planting catalyst (2012)
9. *Christ Church Sparkbrook*, revitalisation (2012)
10. *Redeemer Church Birmingham*, mother-daughter (2013)
11. *The Gate Church*, mother-daughter (2014)
12. *Church Planting Among the Least Reached*, pioneer (2014)
13. *Christ Church Longbridge*, mother-daughter (2015)
14. *St Margaret's Church*, revitalisation (2015)
15. *Nueva Vida*, pioneer (2015)
16. *Second City Church*, multi-site (2016)
17. *Kings Heath Evangelical Church*, revitalisation (2017)
18. *Bloomsbury Hope Centre*, collaborative outreach project (2017)
19. *Open Doors Friendship Centre*, collaborative outreach project (2018)

Data up to date as of May 2019

Find out more at www.2020birmingham.org

2020birmingham.org
church planting for birmingham

REDEEMER
CITY to CITY

Redeemer City to City is a nonprofit organization that prayerfully recruits, trains, coaches, and resources leaders who cultivate gospel movements in global cities primarily through church planting. City to City is based in New York City and works in over 140 global cities throughout Africa, Asia, Australia, North America, Latin America, the Middle East, and Europe. City to City's core competencies are urban church planting, leadership development, and content creation. All of this is done to help bring the gospel of Jesus Christ to cities.

City to City was co-founded and is chaired by Tim Keller. After transitioning out of his position as senior pastor at Redeemer Presbyterian Church, Tim Keller moved into a full-time role with City to City, focusing on ministry in global cities like Johannesburg, Mumbai, London, São Paulo, and New York City. He and City to City's global leaders work together to invest in and pass along what they have learned to a new generation of ministry leaders. Through these endeavors, City to City helps build for and propel movements of the gospel in affiliate networks around the globe.

As of January 2018, City to City has helped start 495 new churches in 70 cities, trained more than 16,000 leaders in city ministry and evangelism, provided resources in 25 languages to help recruit, empower, and develop these leaders, and served 57 gospel networks around the globe.

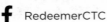

www.redeemercitytocity.com/

f RedeemerCTC

𝕐 RedeemerCTC

◉ RedeemerCTC

▶ youtube.com/RedeemerCTC